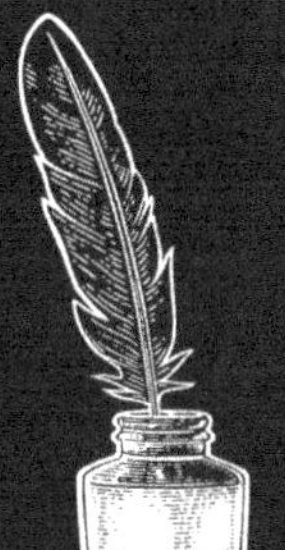

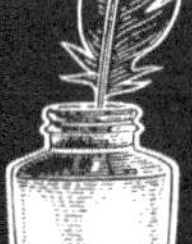

# Calligraphy Practice Workbook

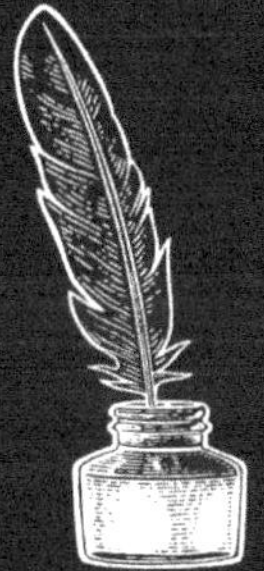

Life Style Daily

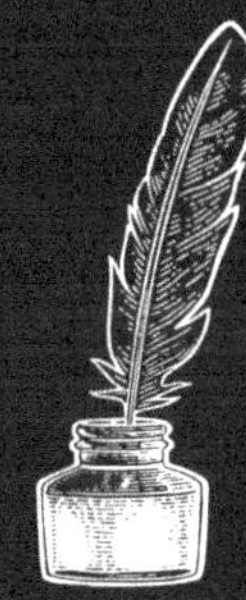

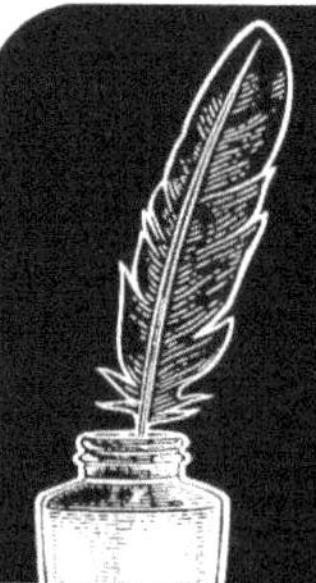

# Typography Basics

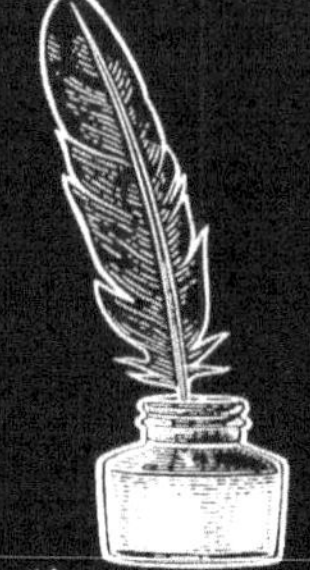

Not to make this overly simplistic, but there are some really basic things that you can do that will set you up for lettering success. In the beginning posture, pen grip and paper might seem underwhelming, but it's really giving yourself the best possible chance at mastering lettering.

## Body

You might be thinking, why does this matter? Well in lettering, or calligraphy (I use the words interchangeably although some purists will say that's wrong. Luckily, they're not the boss of me) the movement of your pen or brush is all important. You need to position yourself in a way that gives your hand and arm the freest range of motion. Which means it's incredibly hard to letter and host a dance party at the same time.

Try sitting at a desk or dining room table or some place where your feet can be flat on the ground and there's a hard surface in front of you. For good lettering you'll be moving your whole arm so it's good practice to use your non-dominant hand to hold the paper in place. This will give you greater control.

## Pen

When holding your pen (or marker or paint brush or whatever fancy thing you've worked out) you want a moderate grip. Something firm enough it won't slip out of your hand but loose enough to do swirls and loops and change the pressure frequently. More on that later.

The most important thing about your pen is that it must be held at an angle. Even a brush pen is still essentially a brush and if you're going to take advantage of the brush strokes you'll need to take advantage of the actual brush. If you use it just straight up and down it's impossible to tell the difference between your soft up strokes and your strong downstrokes. You'll figure it all out, I promise.

This is a new skill, don't get discouraged if you don't get it right away. I promise you didn't pick up walking on the first try, and you fell down a lot. Thank God your parents didn't take one look at your pitiful attempts and decide that walking just isn't for you. They let you get up and keep trying again. Do that here and you'll see big results in your mindset, and probably your lettering too!

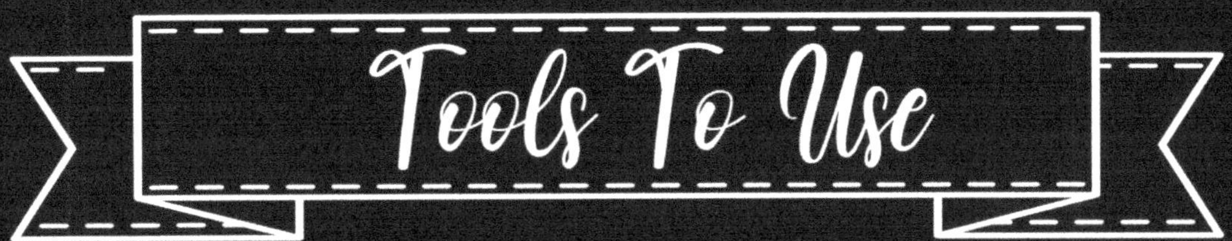


If you so choose, you can go down the crafty crazy rabbit hole and probably spend a boat load of money on supplies. If that's your jam, fantastic. For this book we're keeping it simple so we'll only be using the Fudenosuke Pen and a Brush Pen. But some typical options are:

★ **Pencils**
Simple, basic, nearly everyone can find this. It's a solid option.

★ **Pens**
Not sure where to start? Grab a pen. Micron pens look great, but you could get fancy with a gel or felt tip pen too and get a good monoline.

★ **Brush Pens**
This is the modern version of that quill thing they used in colonial times. If you're not careful, it could become your new obsession.
Pro tip is to avoid starting with a large and soft brush pen because it's harder to control when you're still also trying to figure out your arm movements and such.

★ **Watercolors**
Yep. Real art time. They work great and you can switch up brushes at your whim for varied results. Get experimental, it's fun!

★ **Chalk**
There are markers you can buy and before you know it you'll be a chalk lettering genius. It looks amazeballs and everyone loves a beautiful sandwich board on the sidewalk.

★ **Paper**
We've set up this book that you can use the given space but if you want to practice on something you'll want to get some heavy grade card stock type stuff. Thin paper like printer paper is hard to use so you'll want to invest in something heavier.

★ **Fudensosuke Pen**
In this book we're using a fineliner pen for the monoline script.
You can order any one or pick one up at your local crafting store.

★ **Brush Pens**
For our lettering together you can use a brush pen for the brush calligraphy and flourished designs.

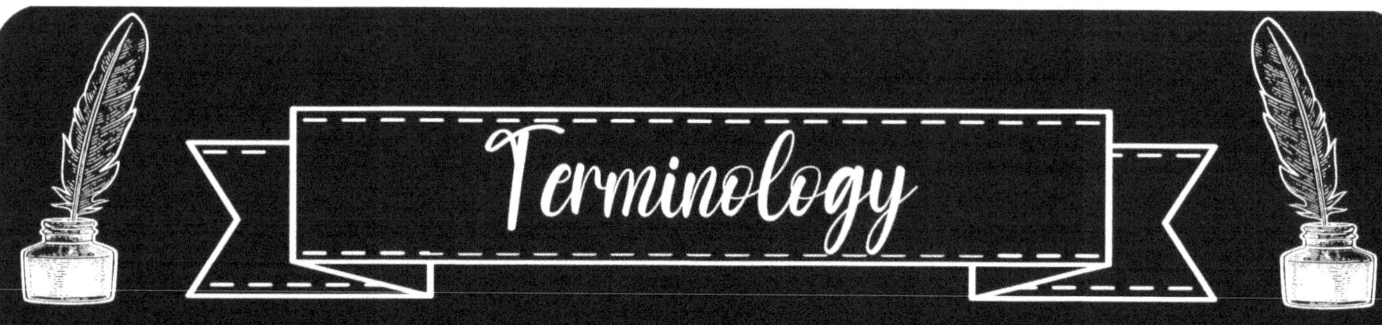


If you're going to learn to letter, we've got to get through a bit of vocabulary words first so don't start skipping pages just yet!

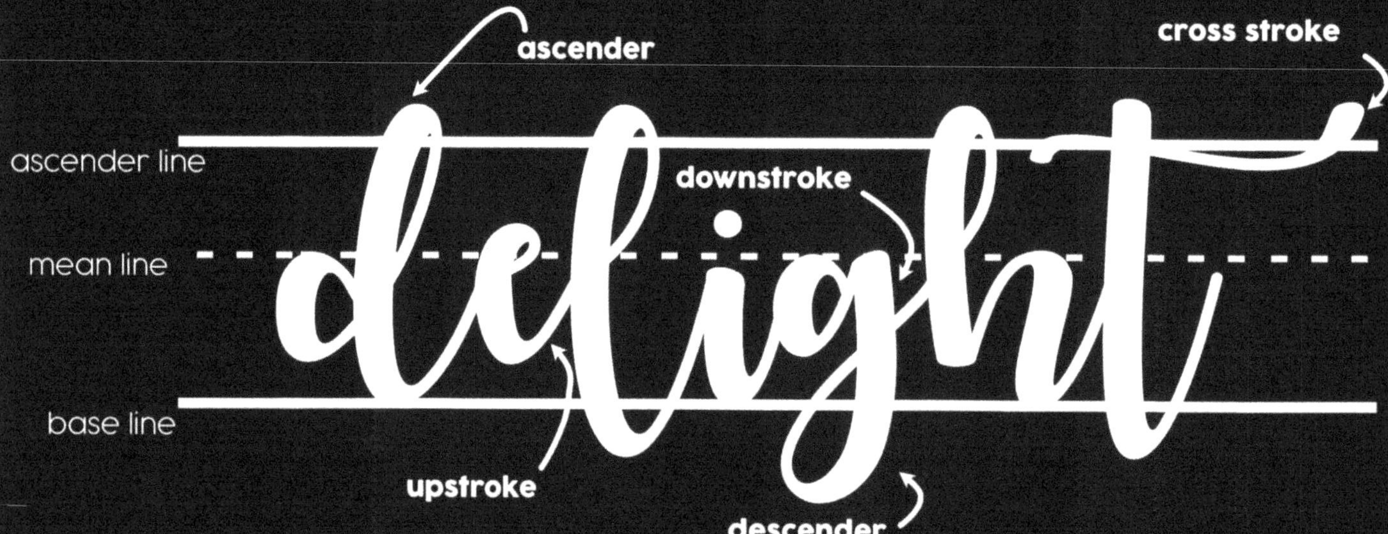


**DOWNSTROKE:** Any movement downward with the writing instrument. These lines are thick!

**UPSTROKE:** Any movement upward with the writing instrument. These lines are thin!

**ASCENDER:** The part of the letter that extends above the mean line (i.e. the top portion of the 't' seen here).

**DESCENDER:** The part of the letter that falls below the baseline (i.e. the bottom portion of letters such as 'g' and 'y').

**FLOURISH:** These are the added strokes and swashes used to decorate or enhance letters.

**CROSSBAR:** Horizontal strokes on letters such as 't,' 'f,' and uppercase 'H'.

**LETTERFORM:** The form or shape of a letter.

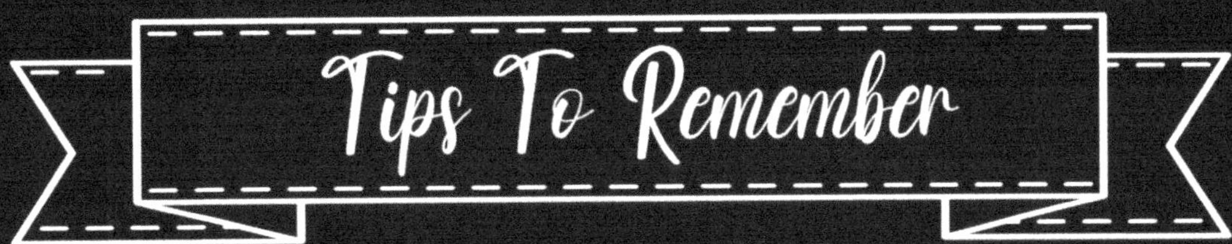


**One:** The most important tip is to write slowly! Think of lettering as drawing each letter, instead of just writing each letter.

**TWO:** Start with pencil. You can draw and erase as you fine tune your letters!

**THREE:** Pick up your pen in between strokes. Unlike cursive, where your pen flows on the paper through the entire word, lettering is made up of multiple strokes.

**FOUR:** As mentioned, in calligraphy down strokes are always thicker.

**FIVE:** Upstrokes are always thinner.

**SIX:** Practice! Master your letterforms first! Then master connecting those letters as you write full words. Once you have mastered connections, practice your composition and design!

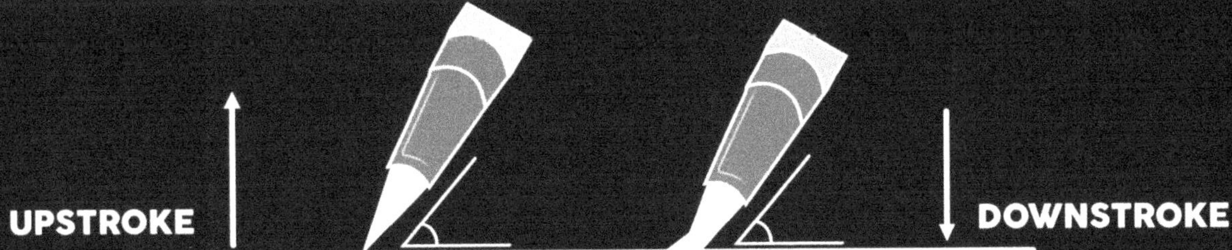


**UPSTROKE** **DOWNSTROKE**

In the next section we will begin to draw our basic strokes & letterforms!
Get those pencils, pens, and brush pens ready! Your lettering journey begins!

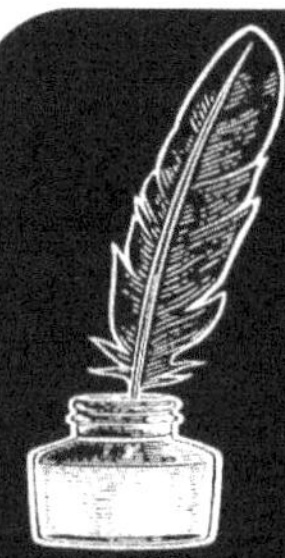

# Basic Strokes

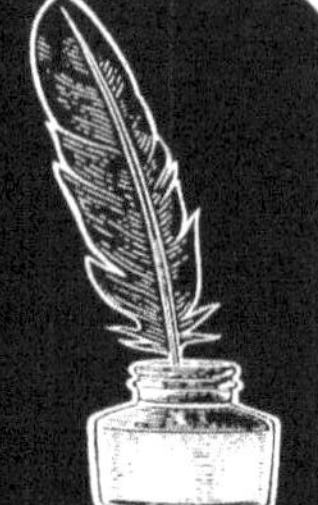

## INTRODUCTION

This is also known as "fake calligraphy". I fell in love with the pretty thick strokes in my head, but in practice I love the monoline. It's faster (I think easier) and definitely channels my inner crafty Pinterest beast. You use essentially the same movements as the previous Brush Alphabet, but you keep a constant pressure as you letter. No thick down strokes here. You can bust out your pencils or regular pens here too, although the smaller tip is what I'm recommending.

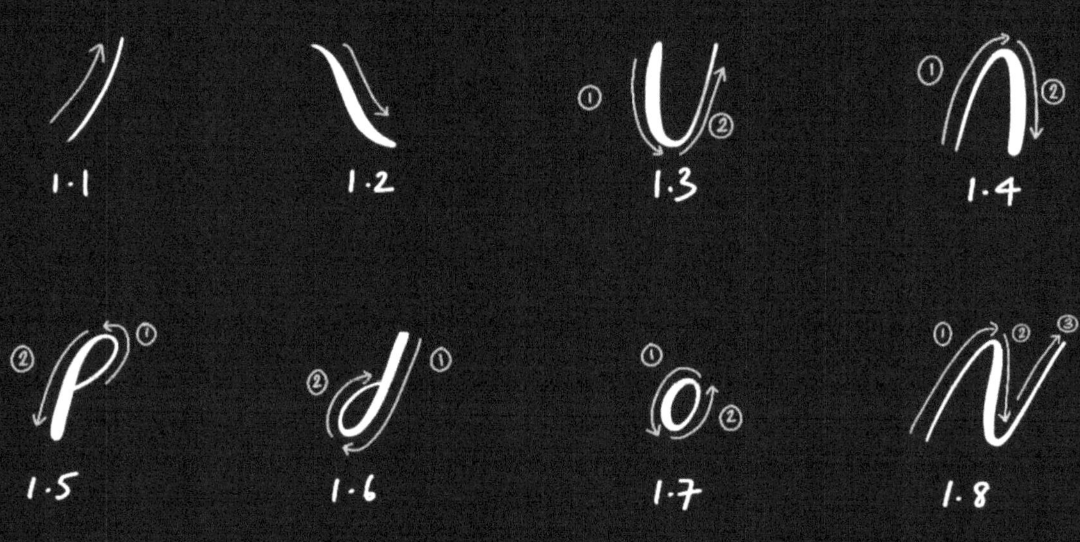


1.1 Upstrokes
1.2 Downstrokes
1.3 Underturn
1.4 Overturn
1.5 Ascending loop
1.6 Descending loop
1.7 Oval
1.8 Compound turn

# Upstrokes

- starts from bottom to top/applied in an upward motion
- thin & consistent
- apply light pressure

# Downstrokes

- opposite to upstrokes
- starts from top to bottom/ applied in a downward motion
  apply heavier pressure
- Start at the top, gradually moving pen down with medium pressure, adding more pressure as you get to the bottom
  ease off pressure at the end

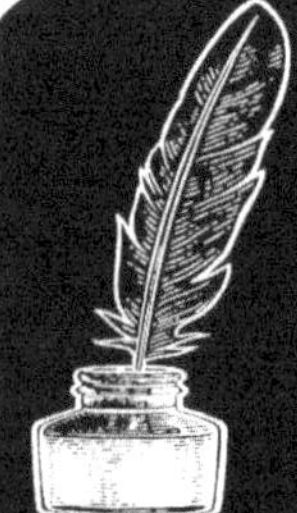

# Under Turn

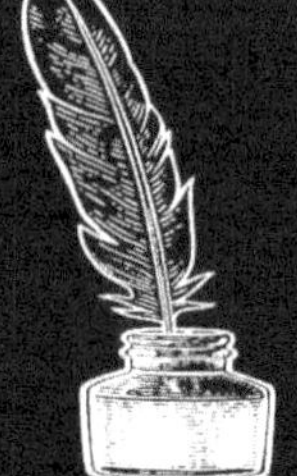

① ②

# Over Turn

- hairline upstroke, transition to thick downstroke

① ②

# Ascending Loop

② ①

# Descending Loop

② ①

# Oral

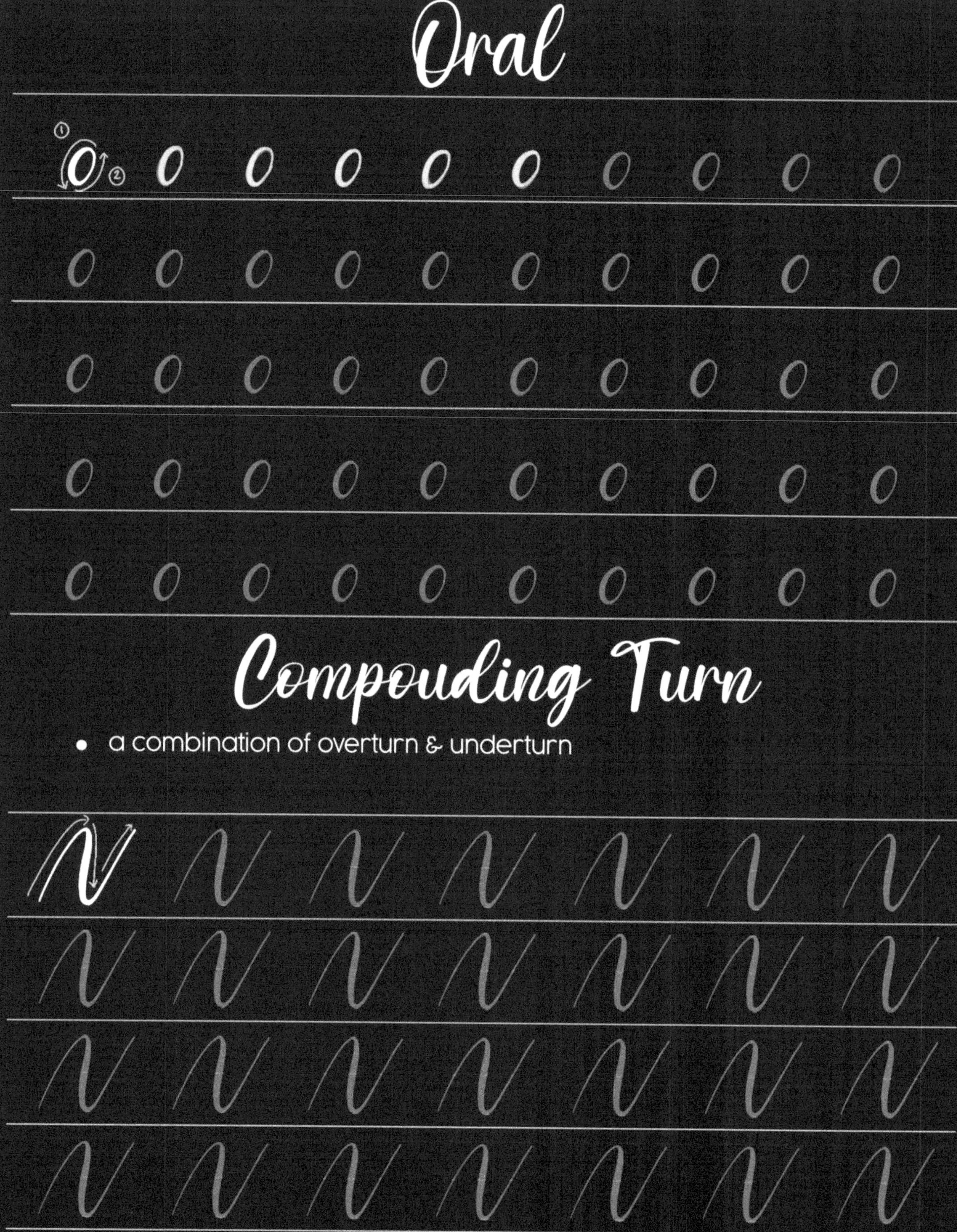

# Compouding Turn

- a combination of overturn & underturn

# Practice Sheet

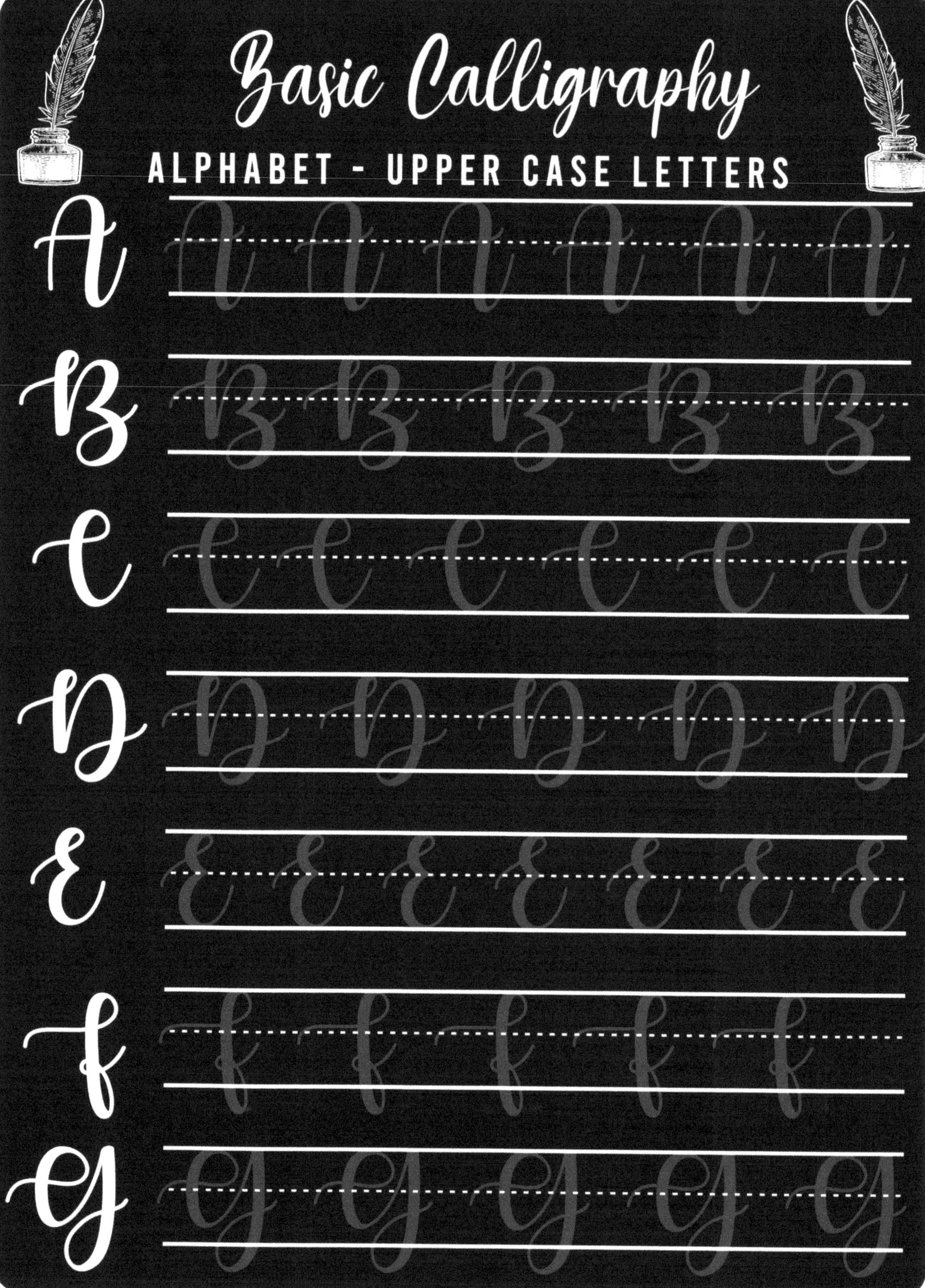
Basic Calligraphy
ALPHABET - UPPER CASE LETTERS
A
B
C
D
E
F
G

# Practice Sheet

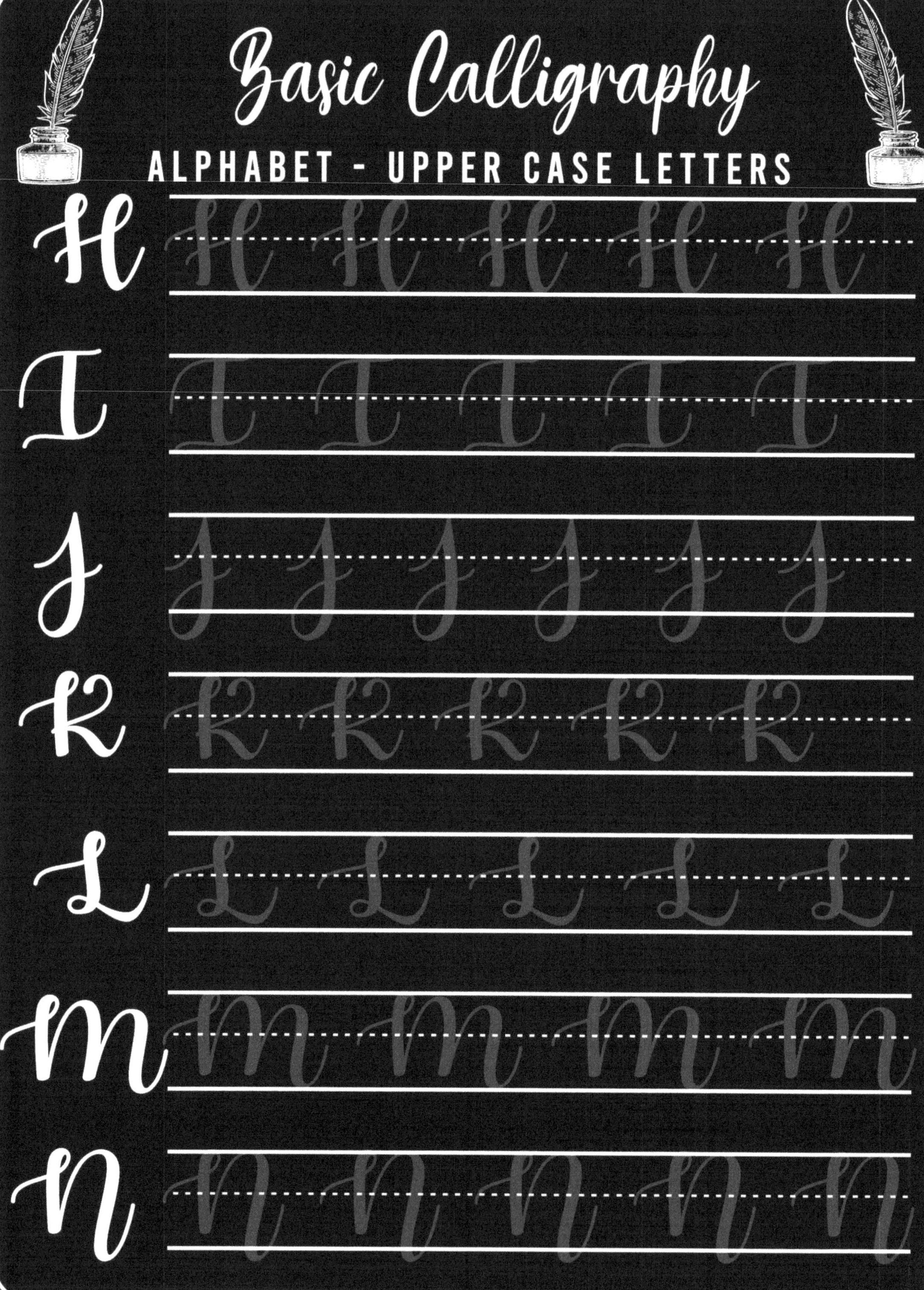
Basic Calligraphy
ALPHABET - UPPER CASE LETTERS
H
I
J
K
L
M
N

# Practice Sheet

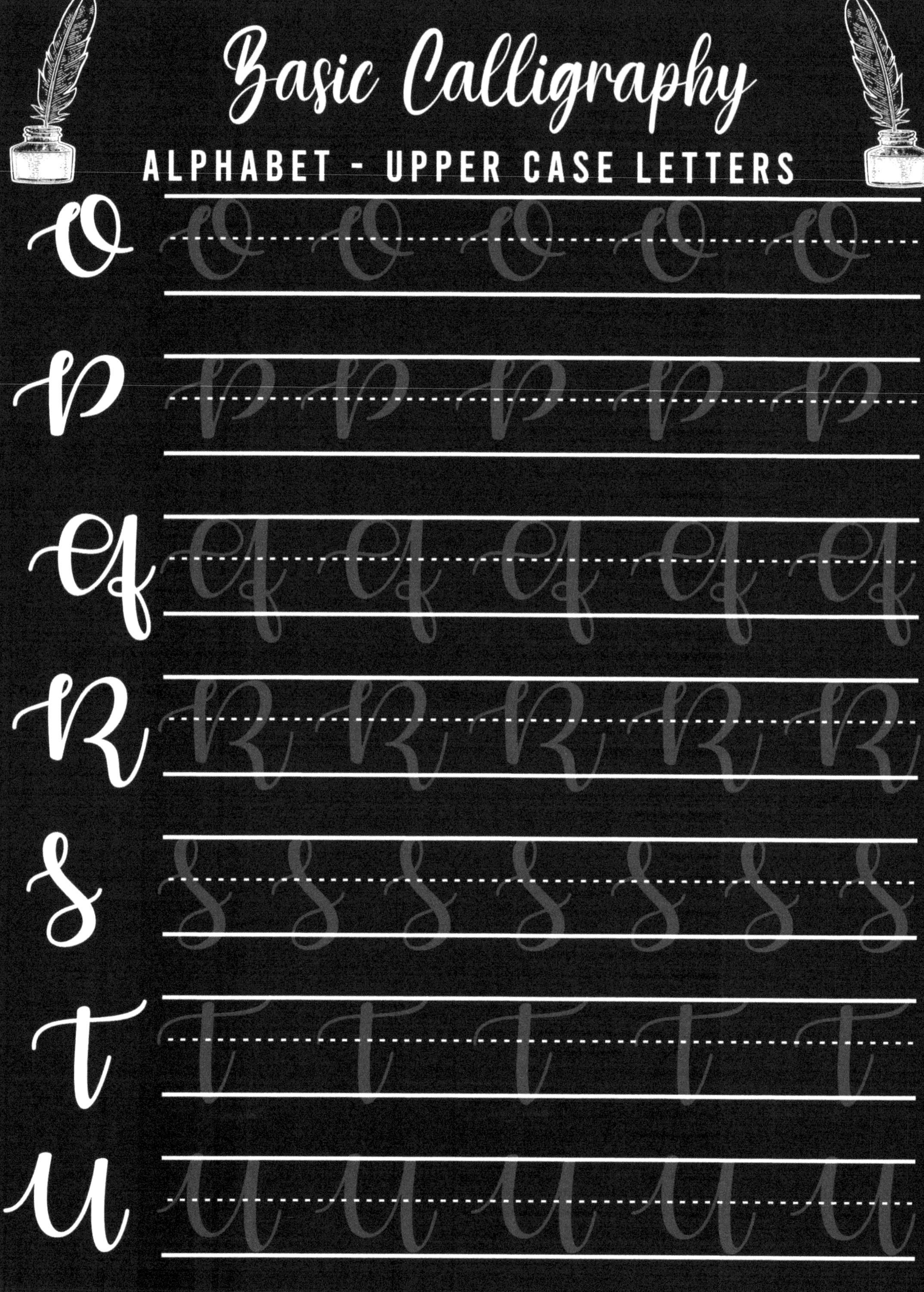
Basic Calligraphy
ALPHABET - UPPER CASE LETTERS
O
P
Q
R
S
T
U

# Practice Sheet

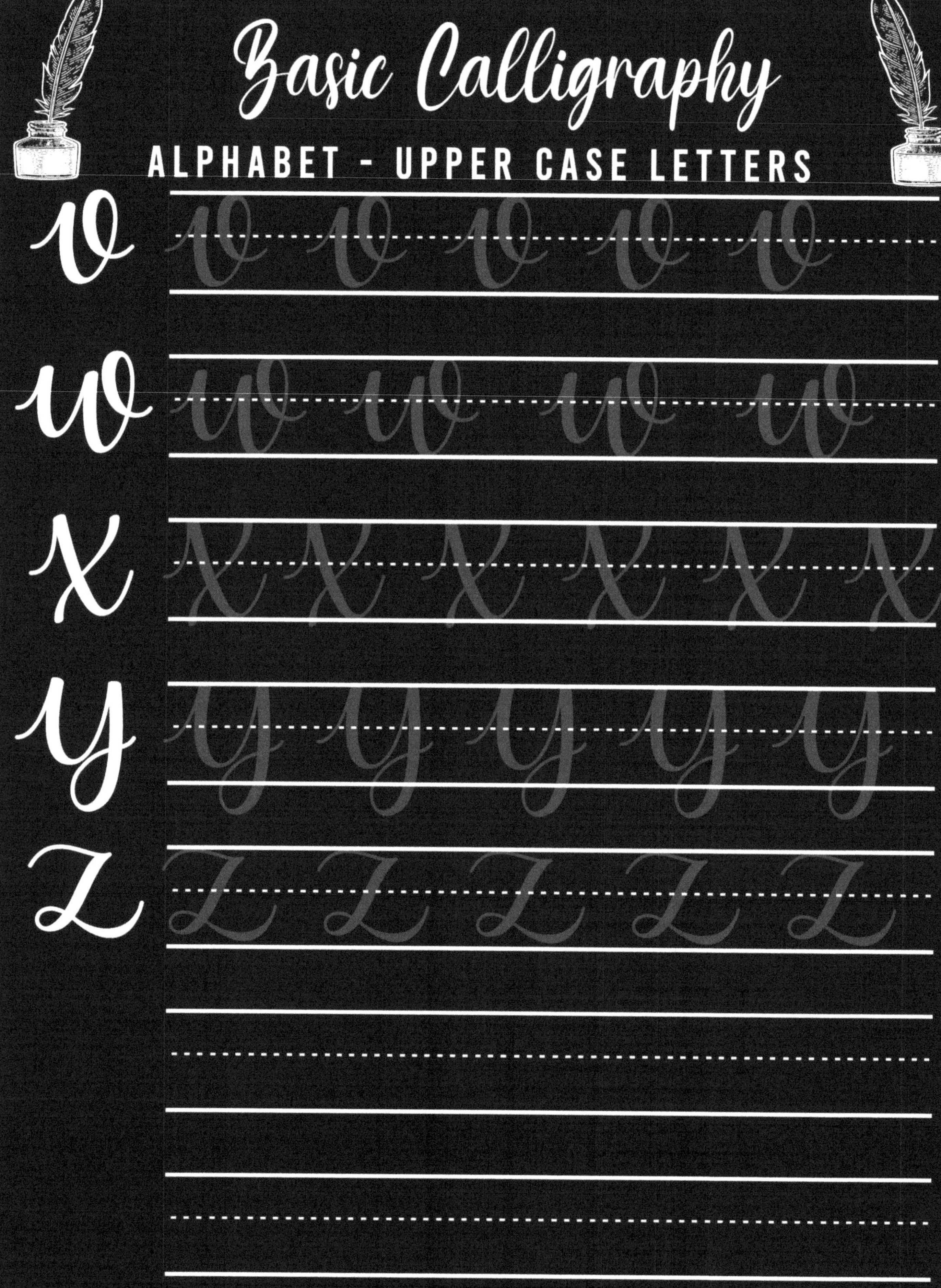
Basic Calligraphy
ALPHABET - UPPER CASE LETTERS
V
W
X
Y
Z

# Practice Sheet

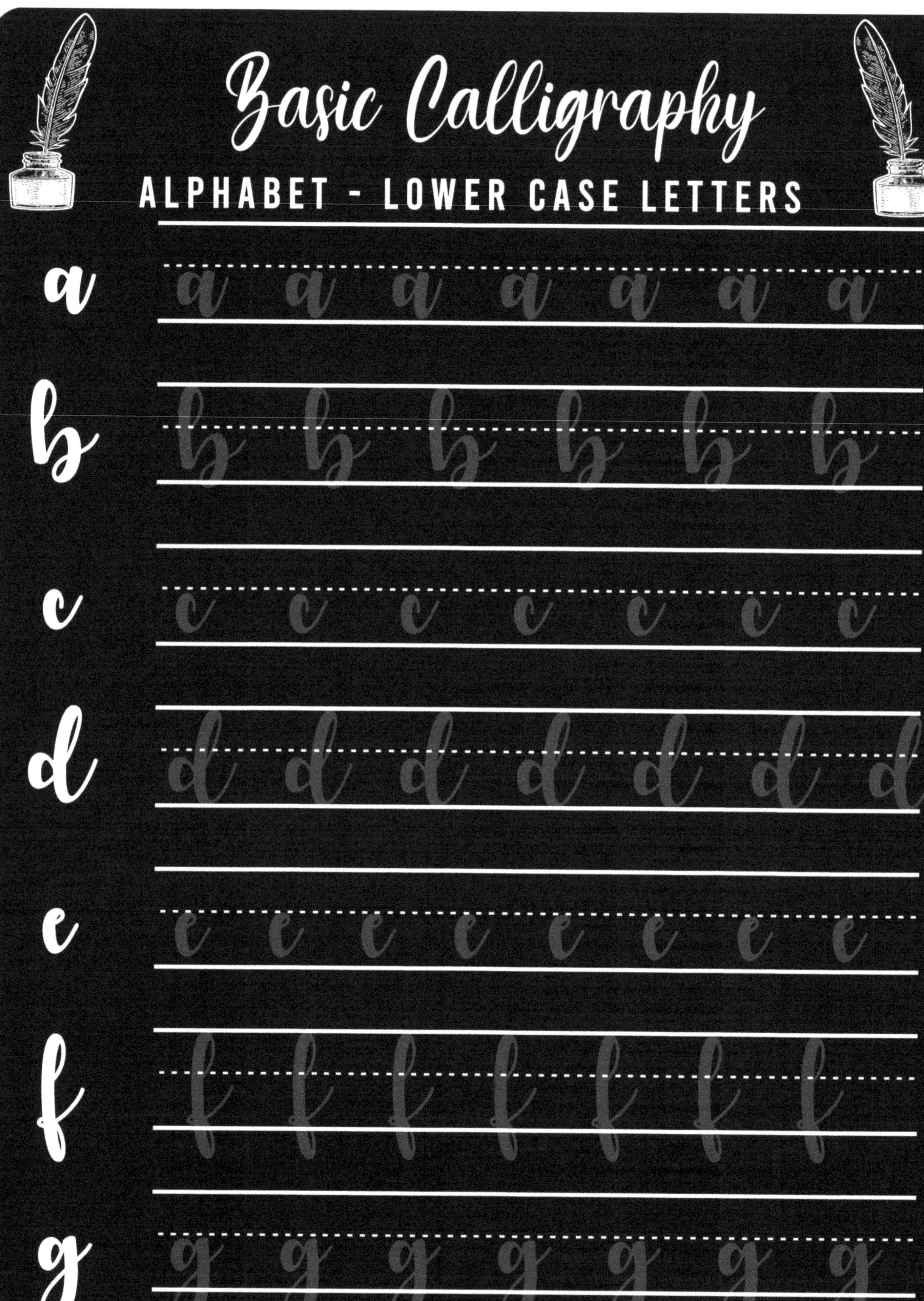
Basic Calligraphy
ALPHABET - LOWER CASE LETTERS
a
b
c
d
e
f
g

# Practice Sheet

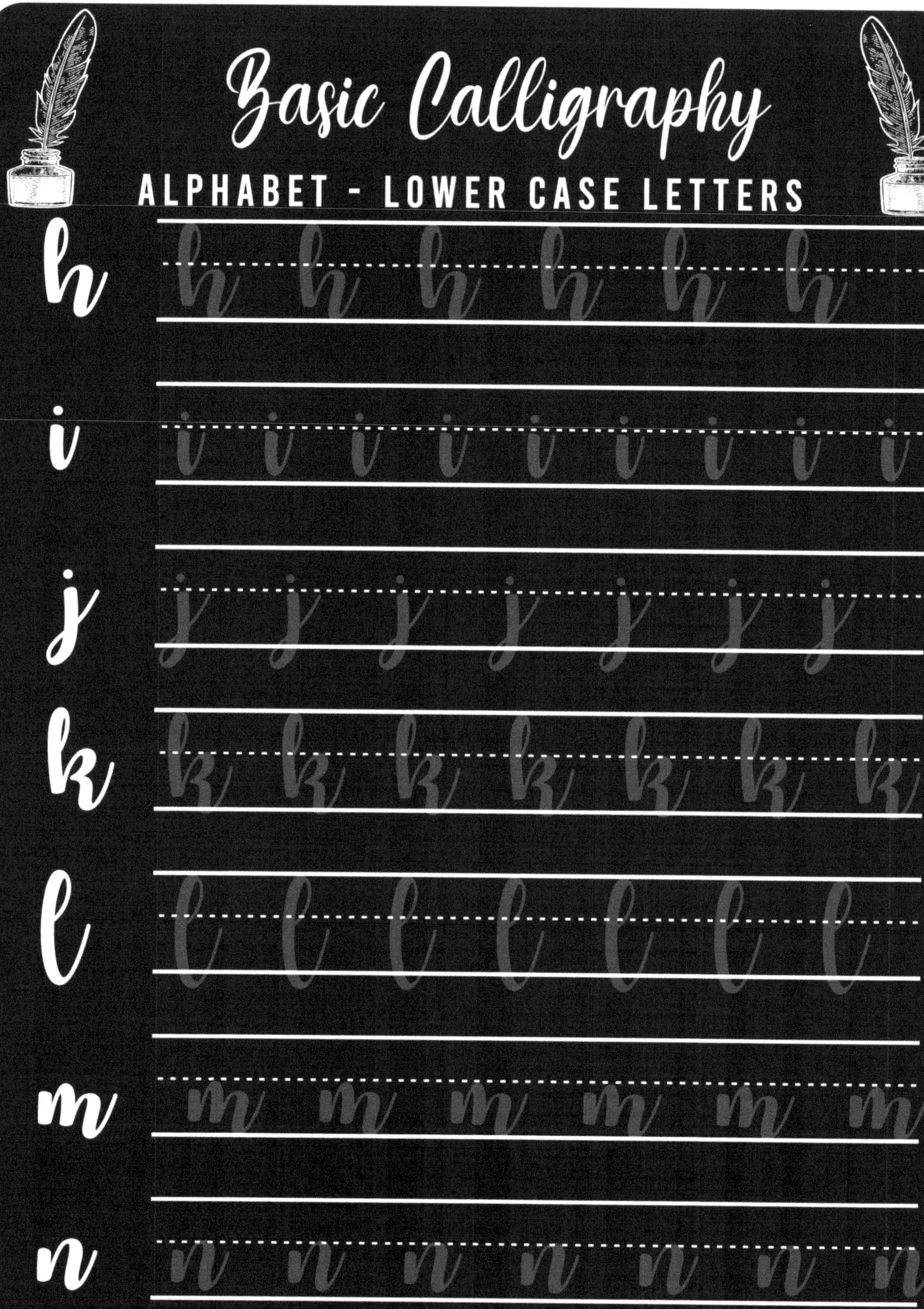
Basic Calligraphy
ALPHABET - LOWER CASE LETTERS
h
i
j
k
l
m
n

# Practice Sheet

# Basic Calligraphy

## ALPHABET - LOWER CASE LETTERS

o o o o o o o o o

p p p p p p p p

q q q q q q q

r r r r r r r r

s s s s s s s s s

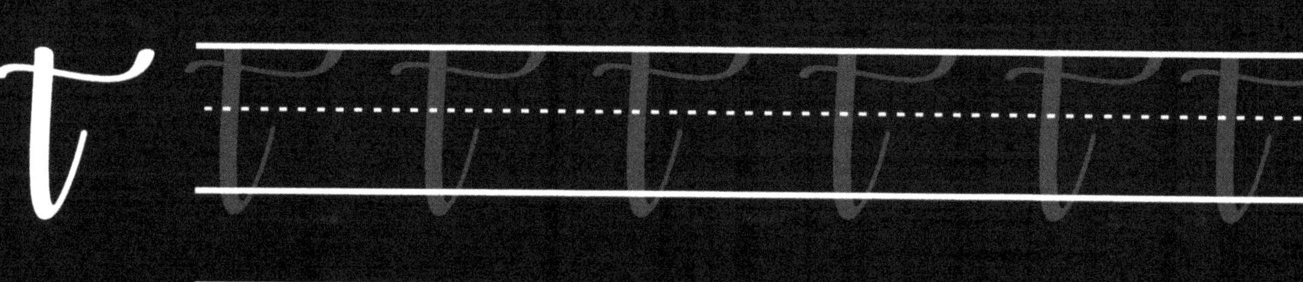


u u u u u u u u

# Practice Sheet

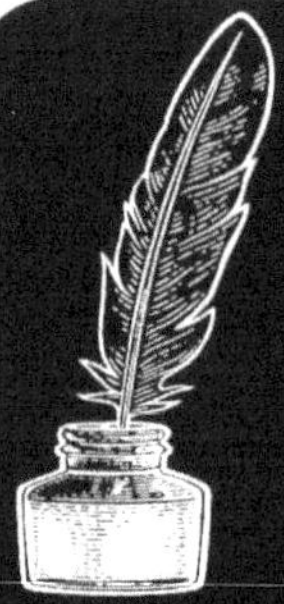

# Basic Calligraphy

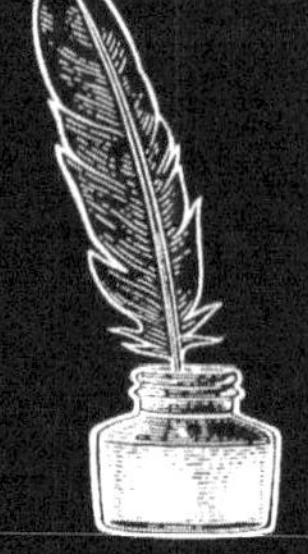

## ALPHABET - LOWER CASE LETTERS

v v v v v v v v

w w w w w w w

x x x x x x x

y y y y y y y y

z z z z z z z z

# Practice Sheet

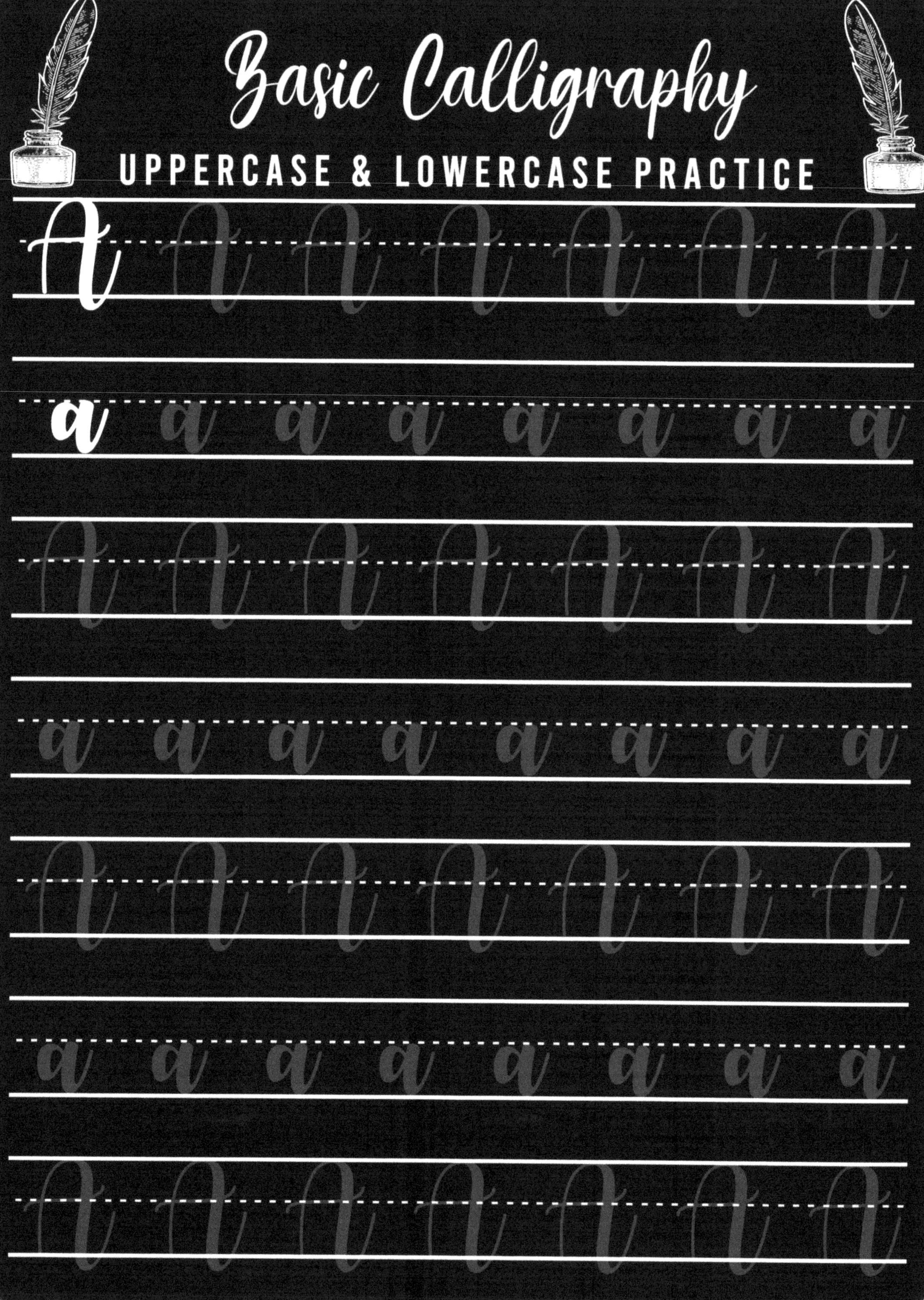
Basic Calligraphy
UPPERCASE & LOWERCASE PRACTICE
A
a

# Practice Sheet

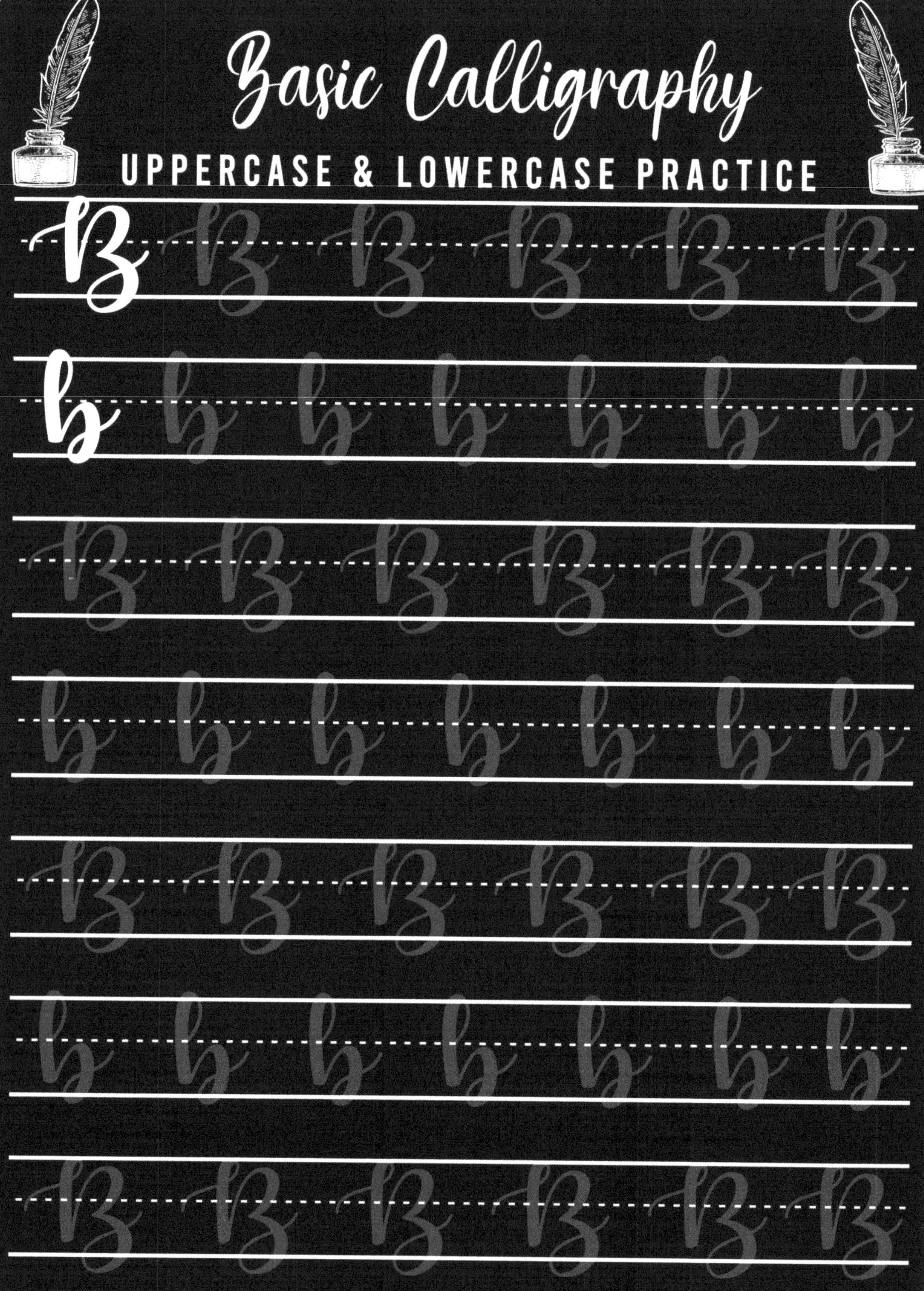
Basic Calligraphy
UPPERCASE & LOWERCASE PRACTICE
B
b

# Practice Sheet

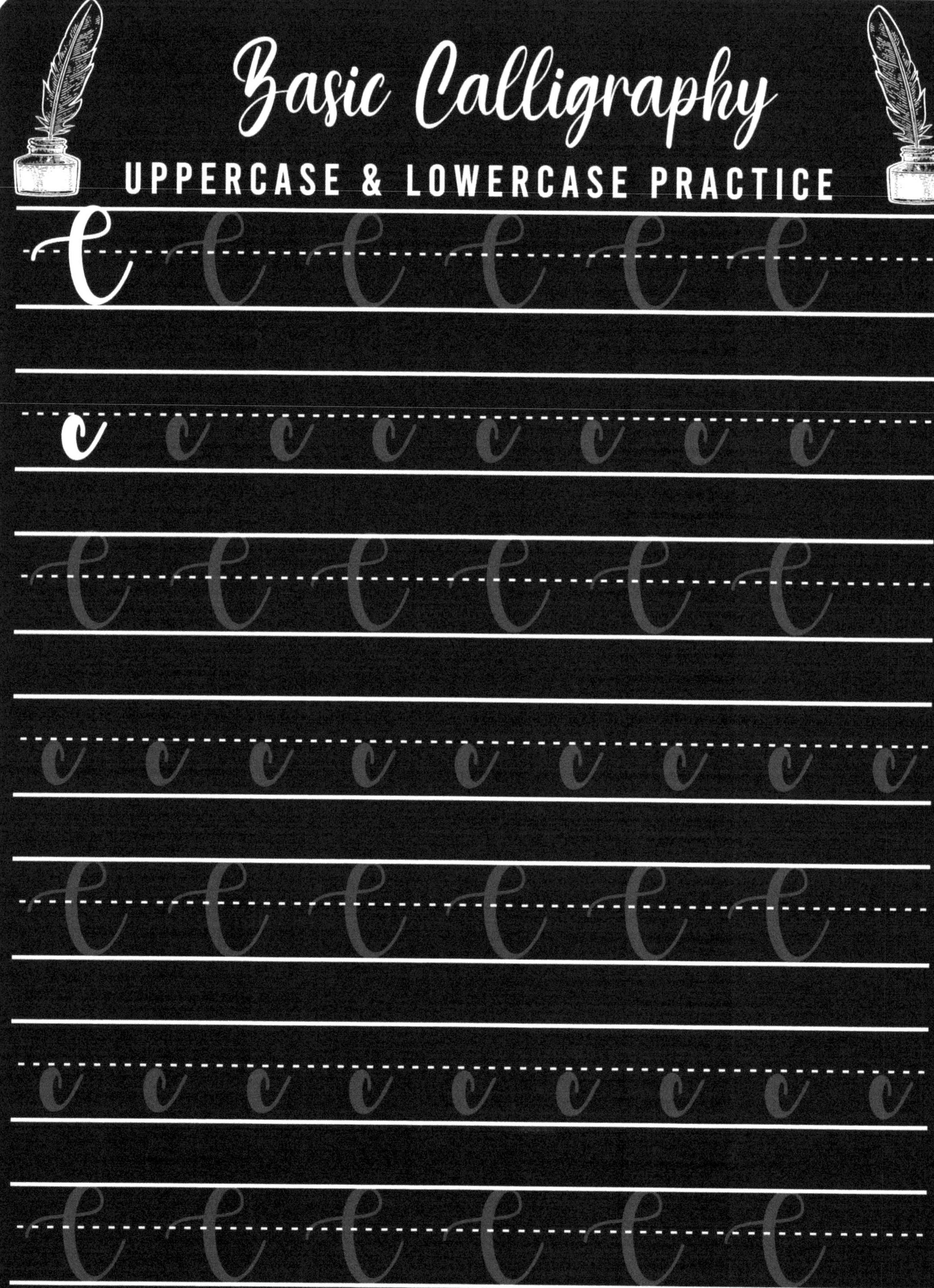
Basic Calligraphy
UPPERCASE & LOWERCASE PRACTICE
C
c

# Practice Sheet

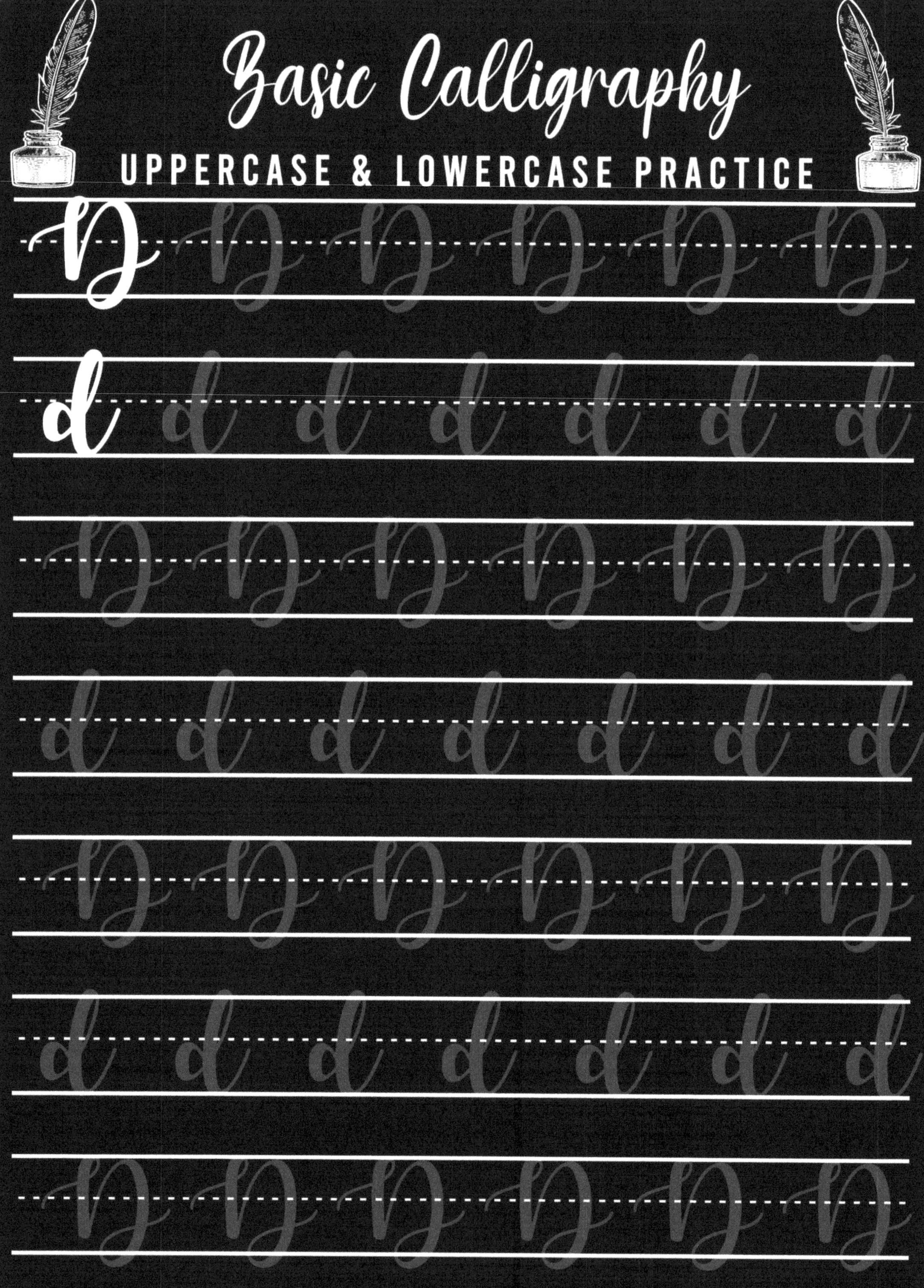
Basic Calligraphy
UPPERCASE & LOWERCASE PRACTICE
D
d

# Practice Sheet

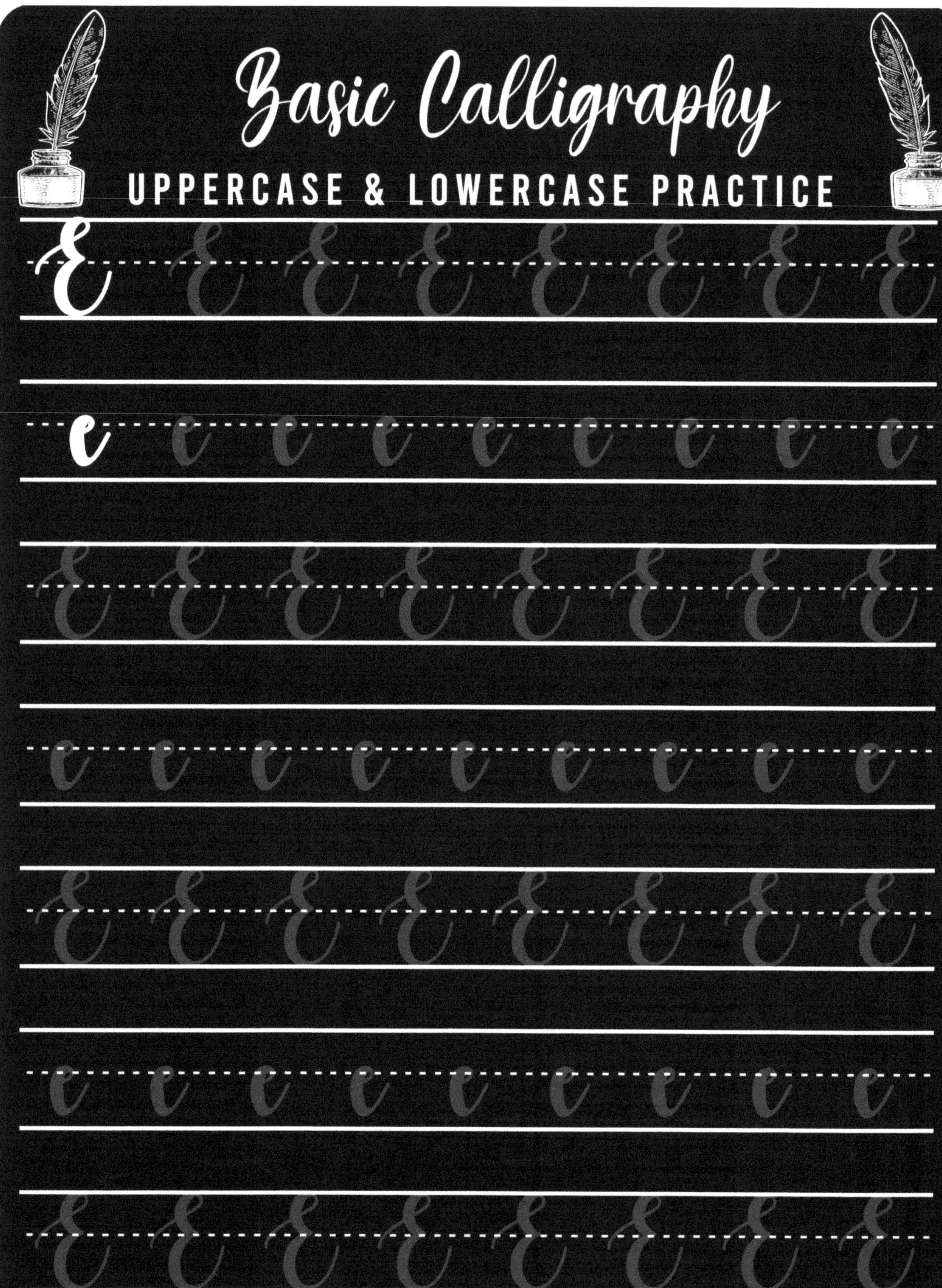
Basic Calligraphy
UPPERCASE & LOWERCASE PRACTICE
E
e

# Practice Sheet

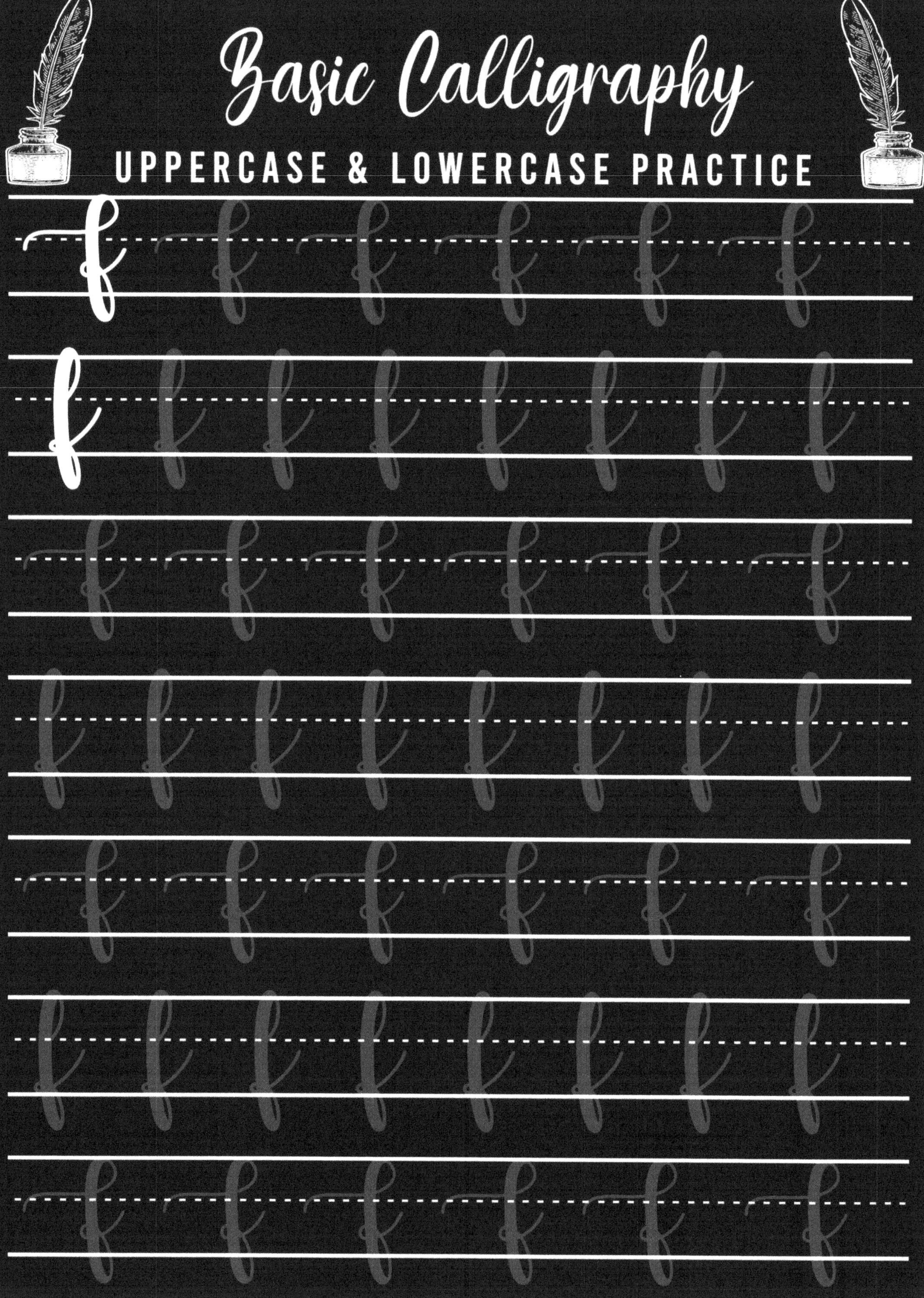

Basic Calligraphy
UPPERCASE & LOWERCASE PRACTICE
f
f

# Practice Sheet

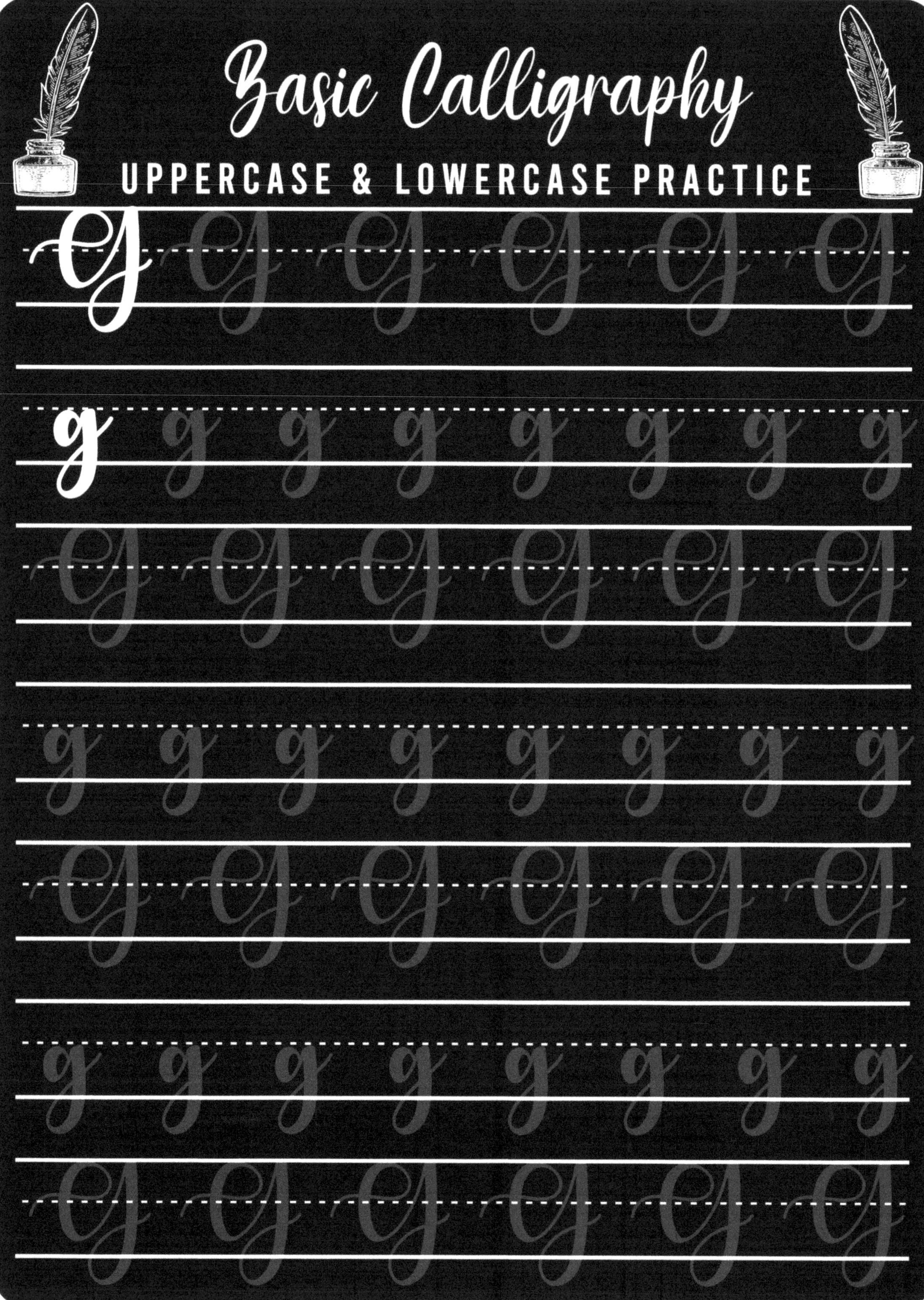
Basic Calligraphy
UPPERCASE & LOWERCASE PRACTICE

# Practice Sheet

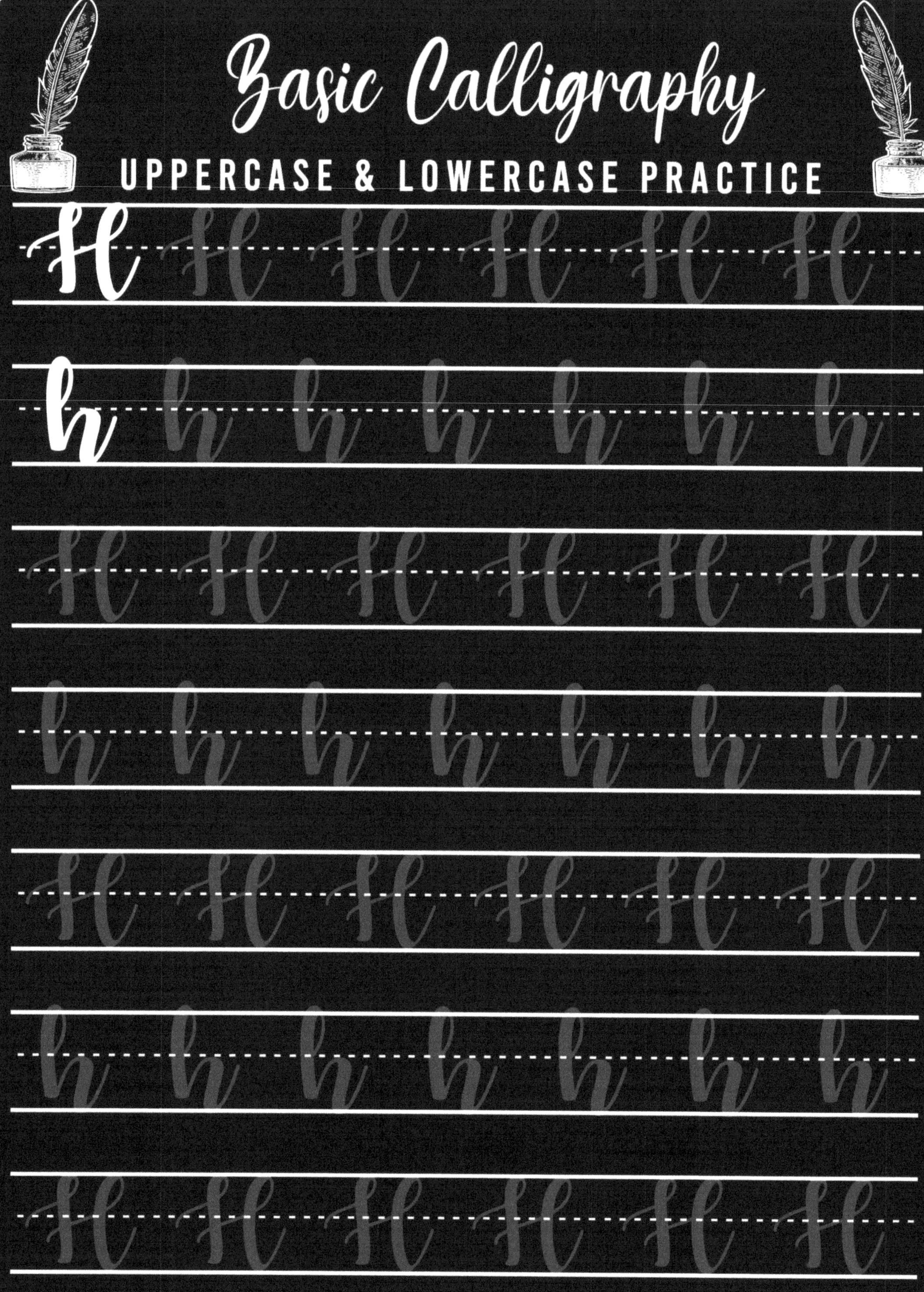
Basic Calligraphy
UPPERCASE & LOWERCASE PRACTICE
H
h

# Practice Sheet

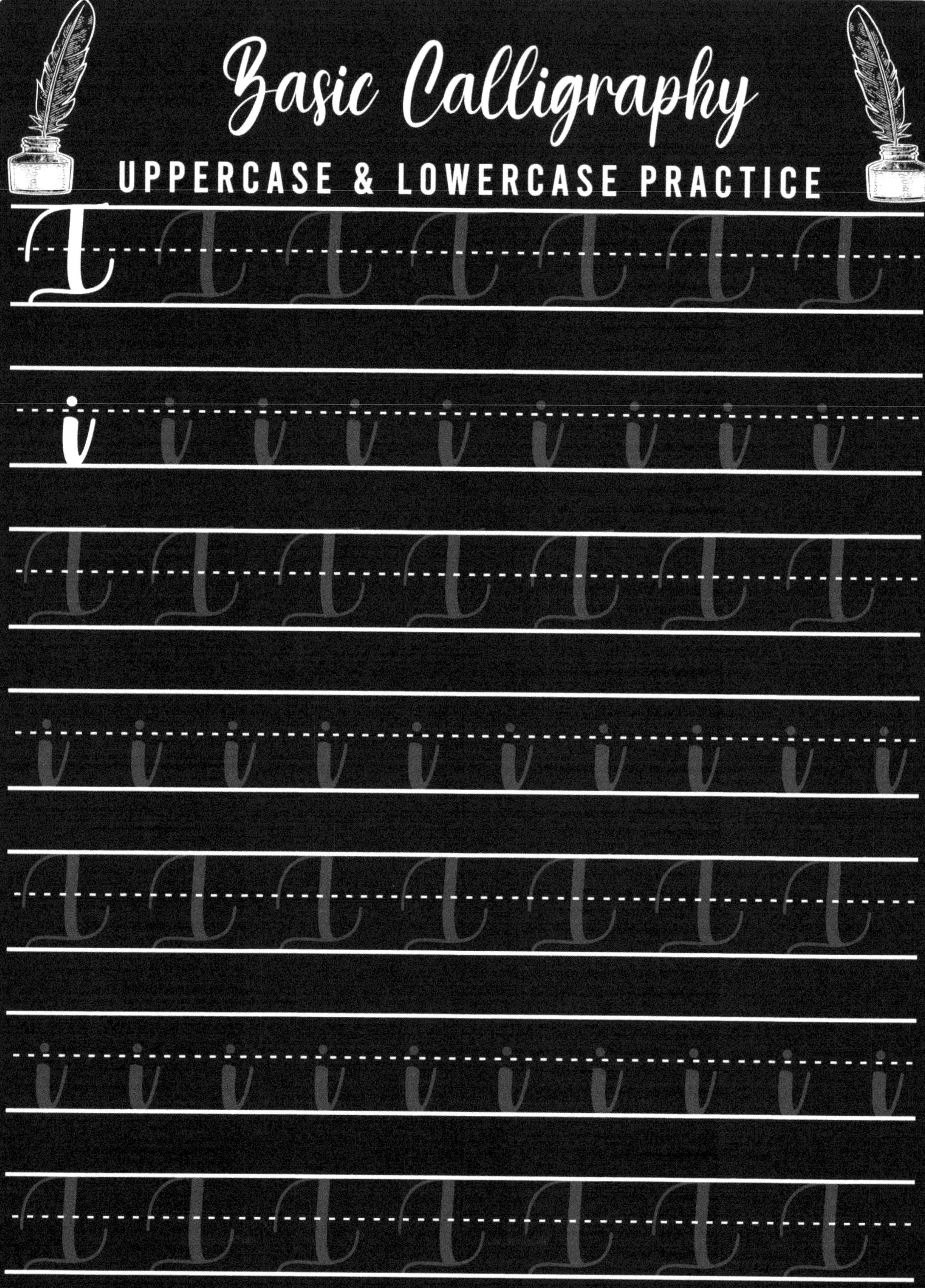
Basic Calligraphy
UPPERCASE & LOWERCASE PRACTICE
I
i

# Practice Sheet

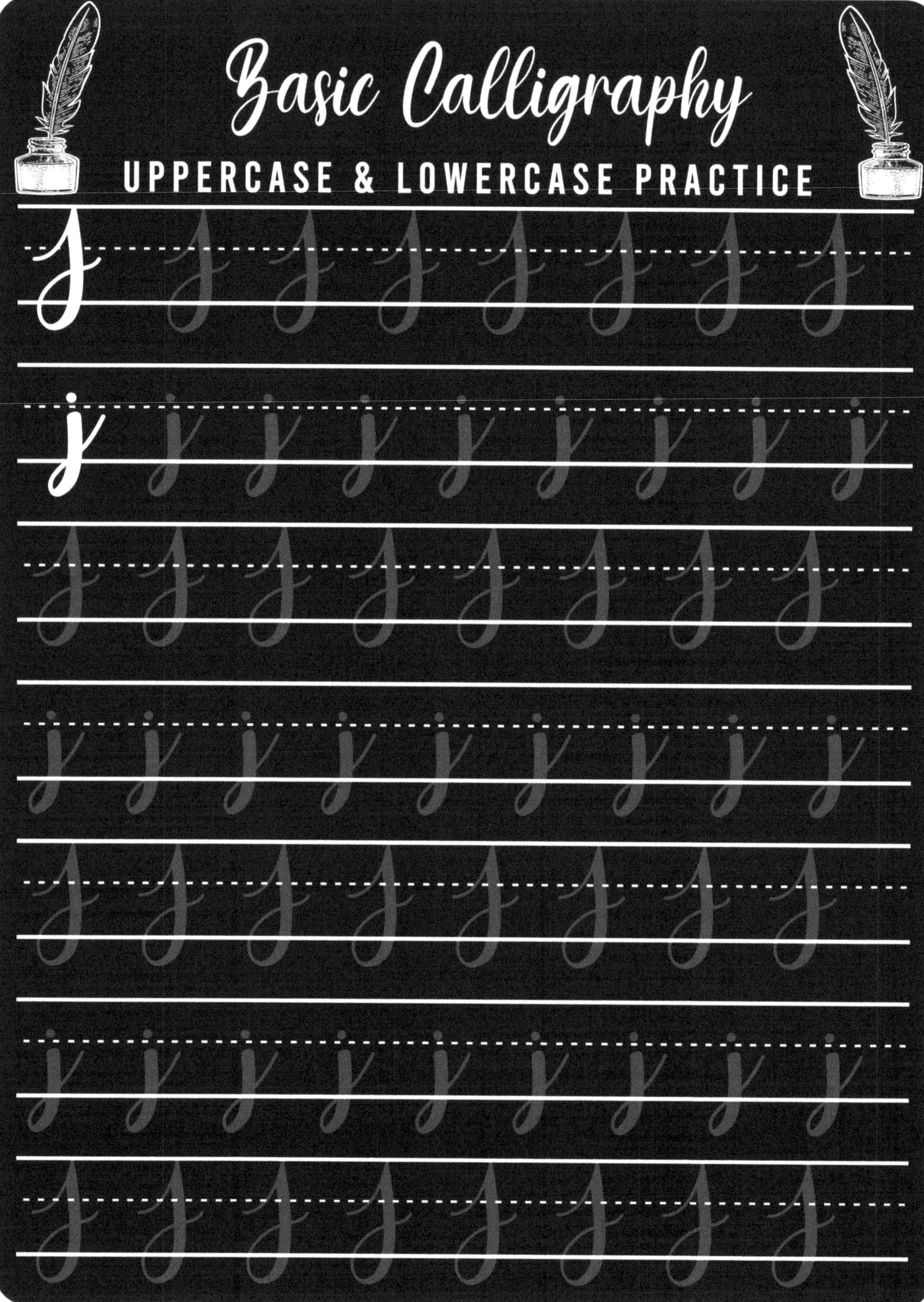
Basic Calligraphy
UPPERCASE & LOWERCASE PRACTICE
J
j

# Practice Sheet

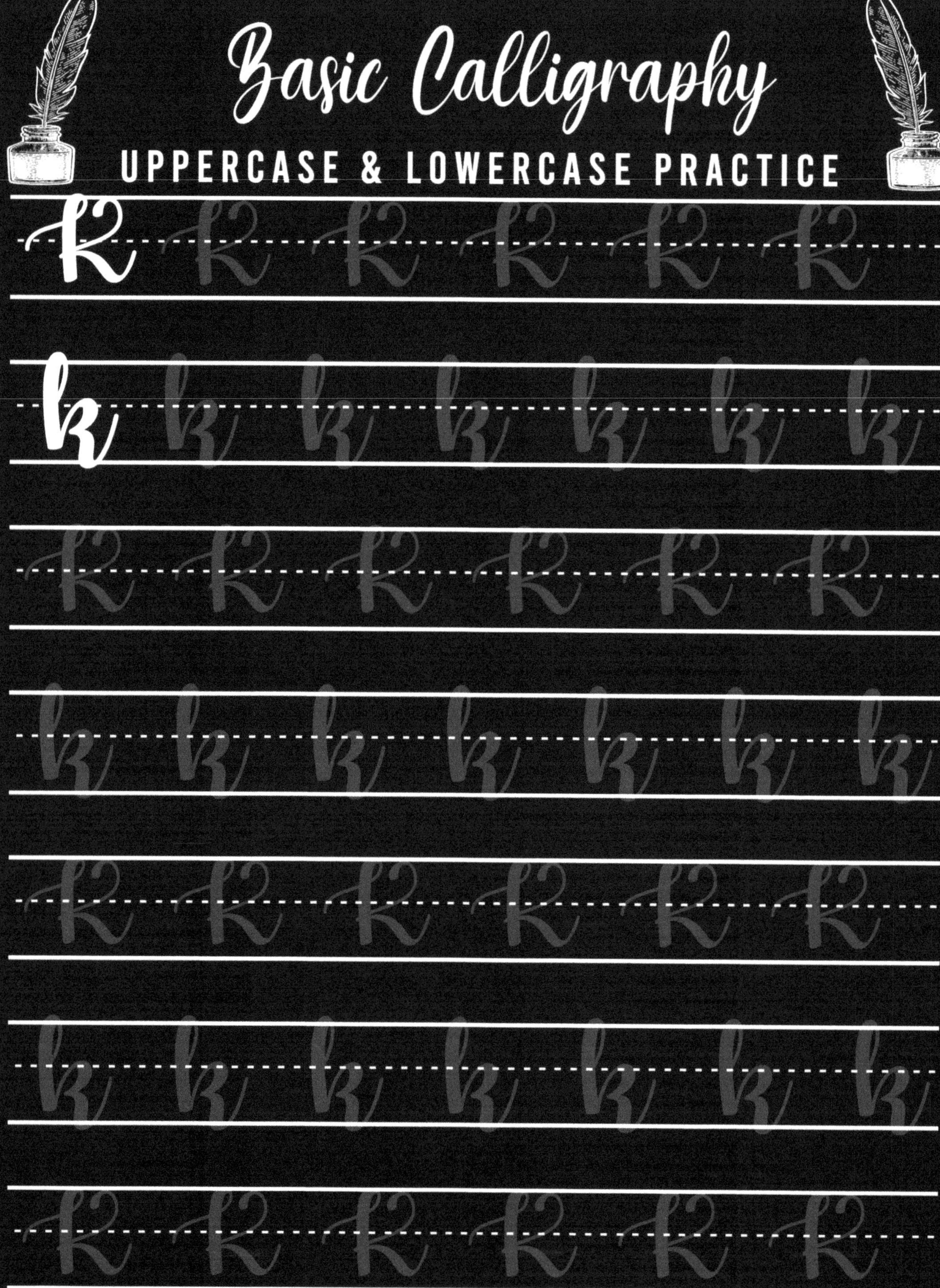
Basic Calligraphy
UPPERCASE & LOWERCASE PRACTICE
K
k

# Practice Sheet

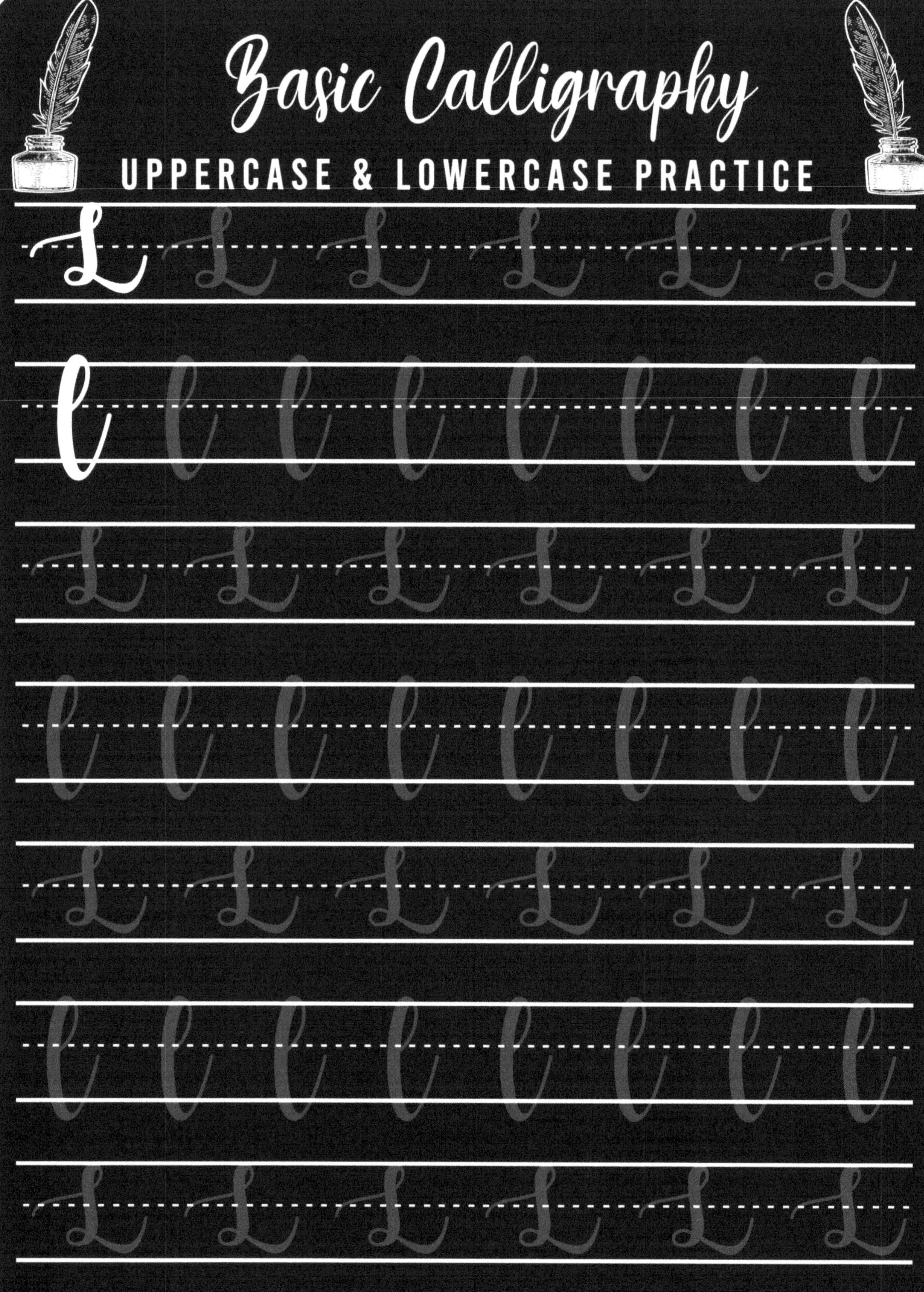

Basic Calligraphy
UPPERCASE & LOWERCASE PRACTICE
L
l

# Practice Sheet

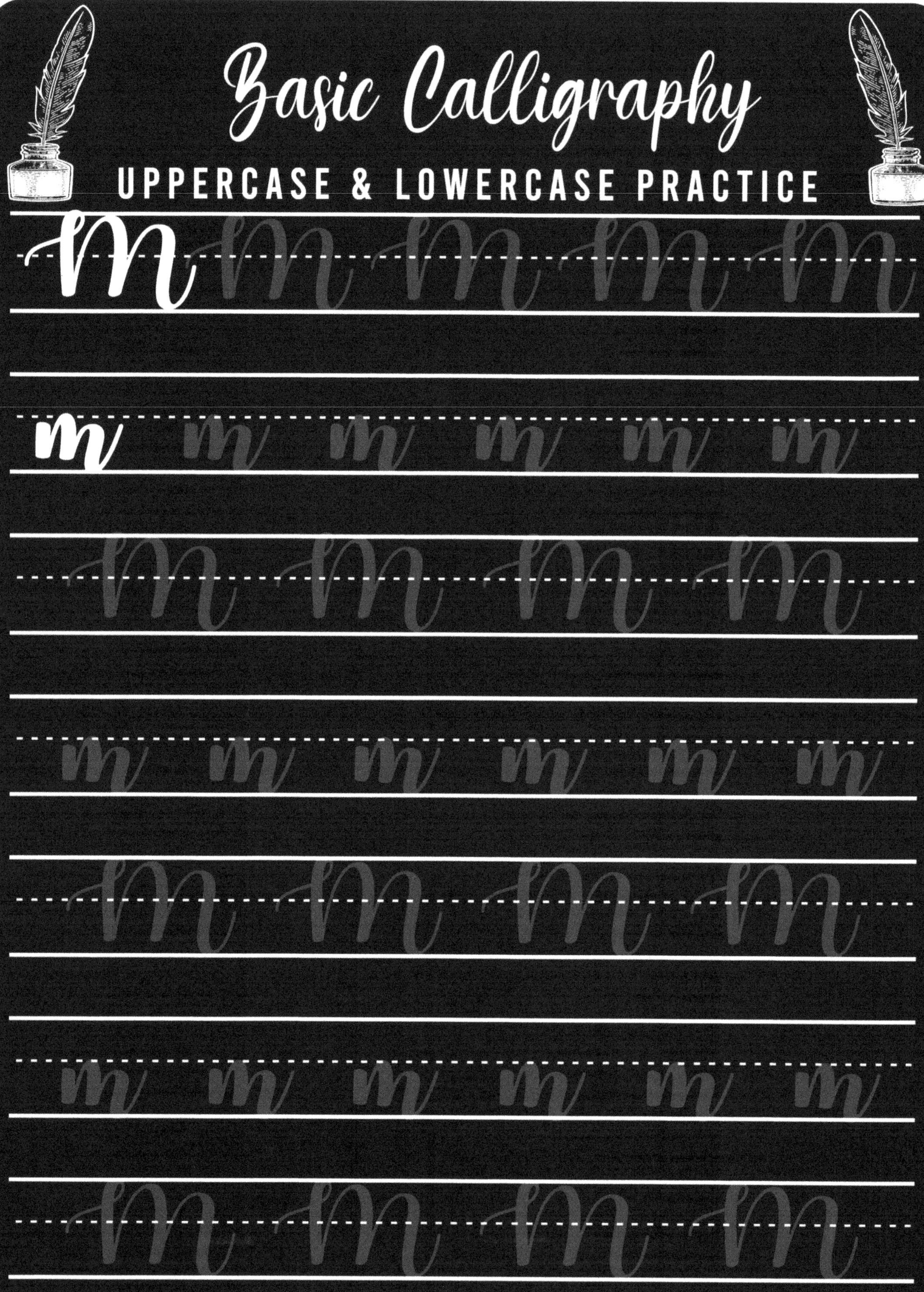
Basic Calligraphy
UPPERCASE & LOWERCASE PRACTICE

# Practice Sheet

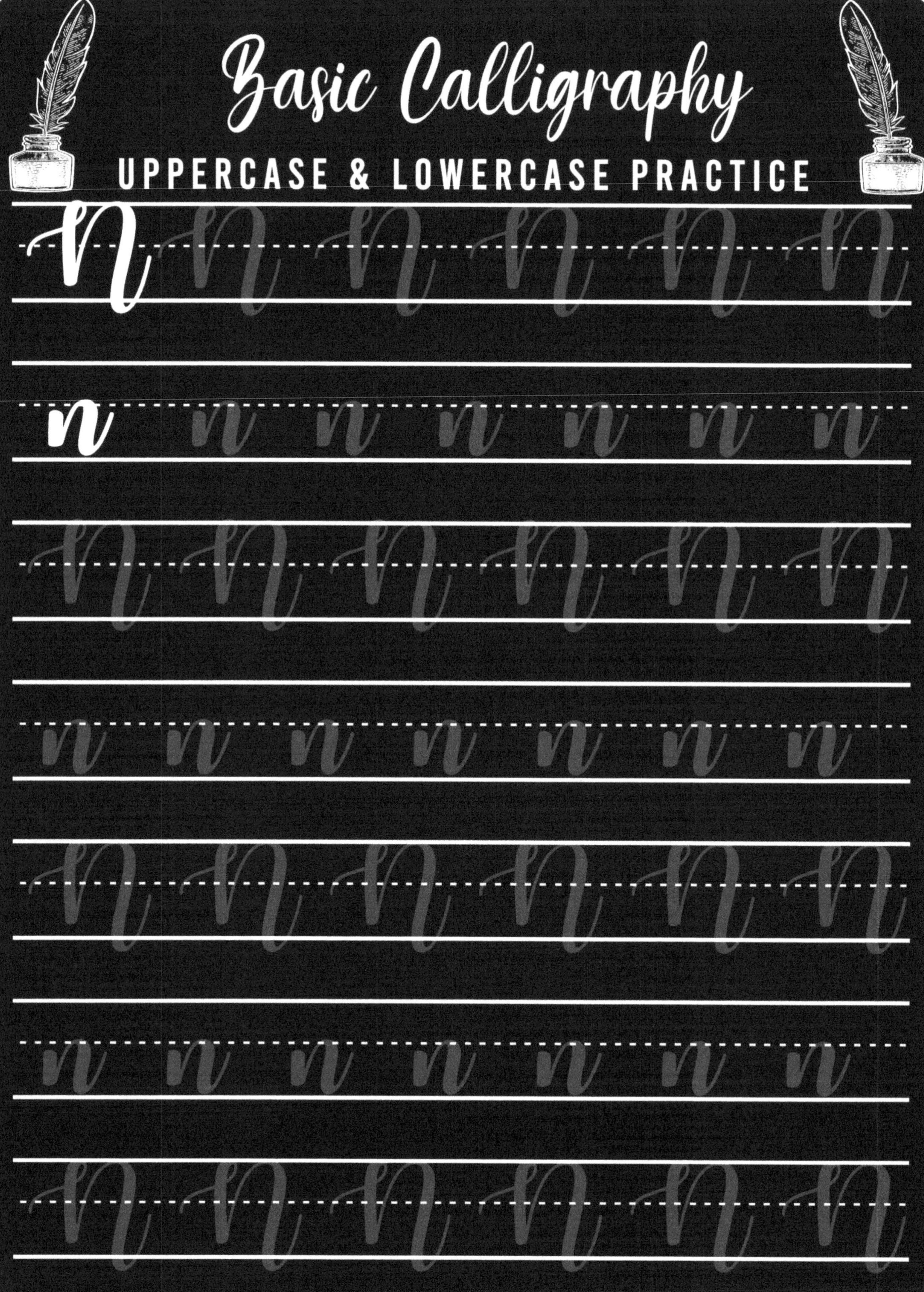

Basic Calligraphy
UPPERCASE & LOWERCASE PRACTICE
N N N N N N N
n n n n n n n
N N N N N N N
n n n n n n n
N N N N N N N
n n n n n n n
N N N N N N N

# Practice Sheet

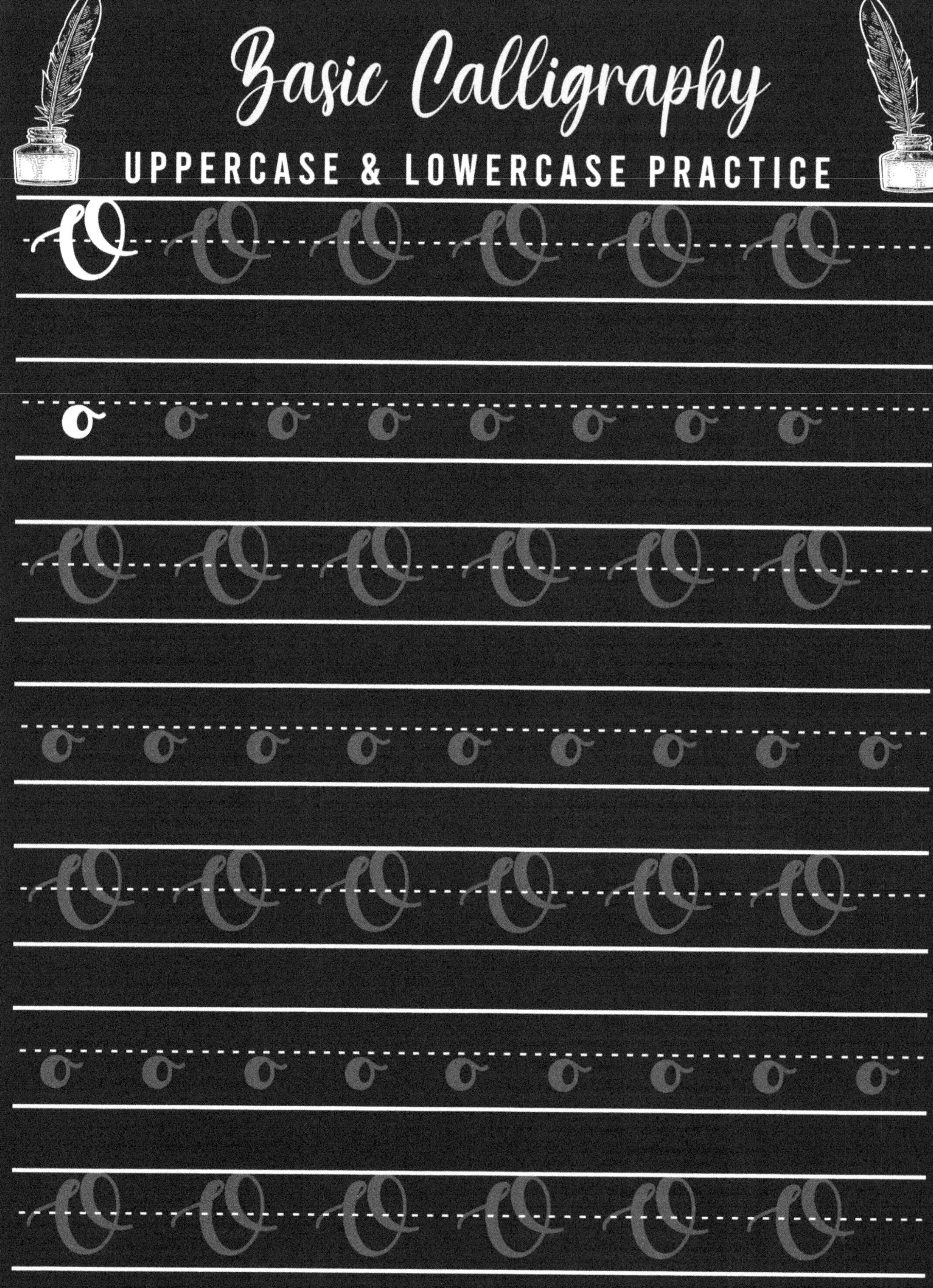
Basic Calligraphy
UPPERCASE & LOWERCASE PRACTICE
O
o

# Practice Sheet

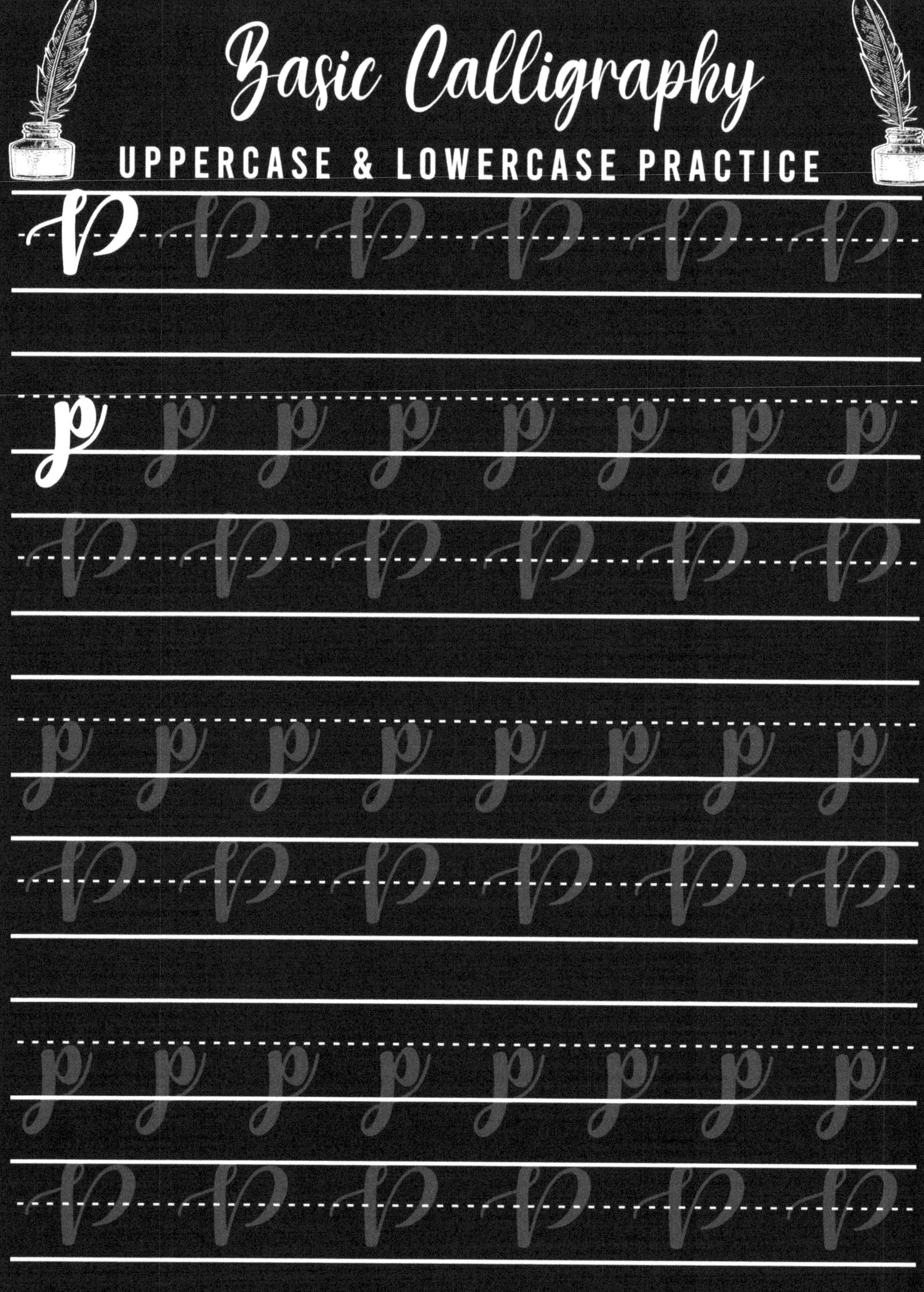
Basic Calligraphy
UPPERCASE & LOWERCASE PRACTICE

# Practice Sheet

# Basic Calligraphy

## UPPERCASE & LOWERCASE PRACTICE

Q Q Q Q Q Q

q q q q q q q q

Q Q Q Q Q Q

q q q q q q q q

Q Q Q Q Q Q

q q q q q q q q

Q Q Q Q Q Q

# Practice Sheet

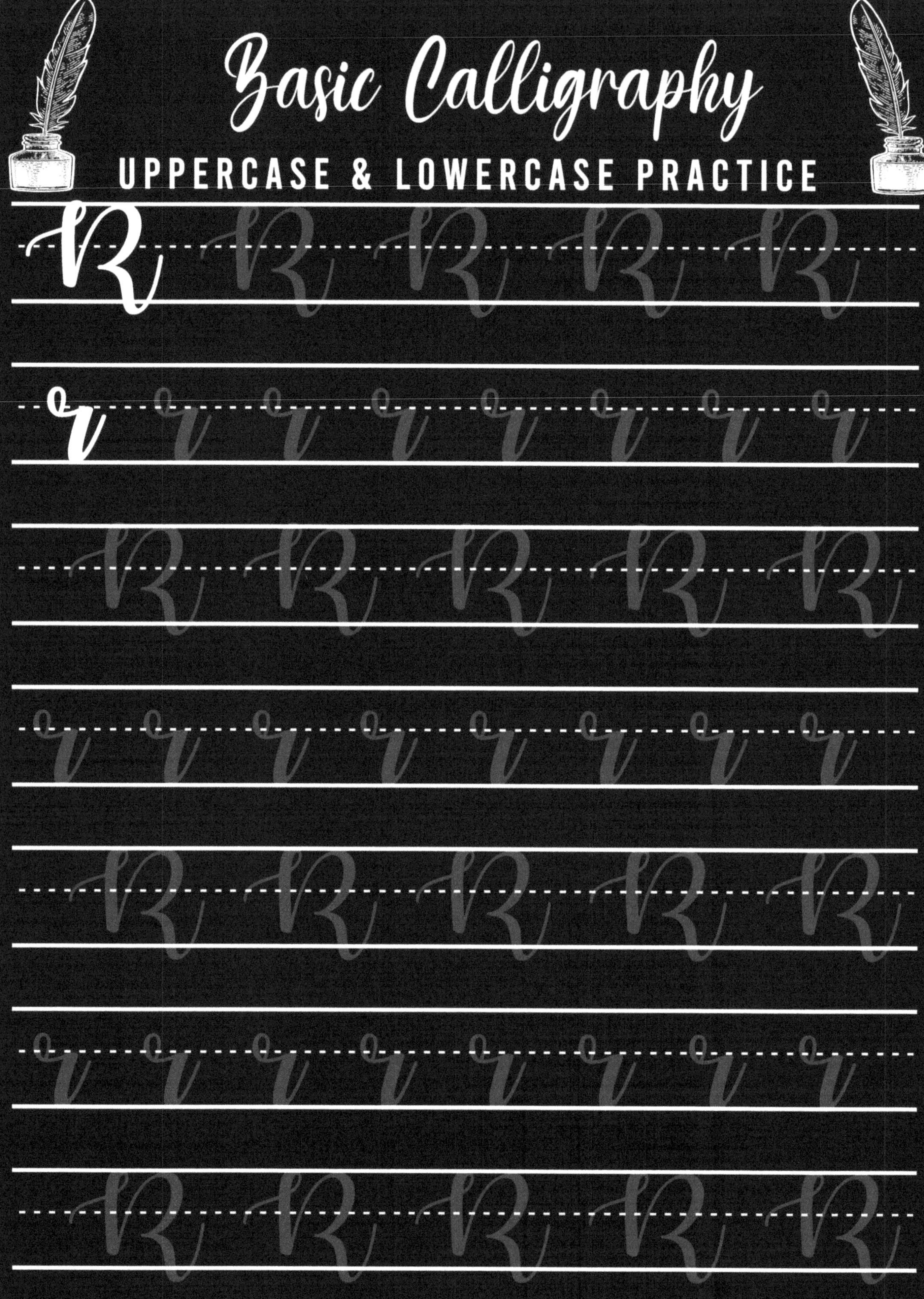
Basic Calligraphy
UPPERCASE & LOWERCASE PRACTICE

# Practice Sheet

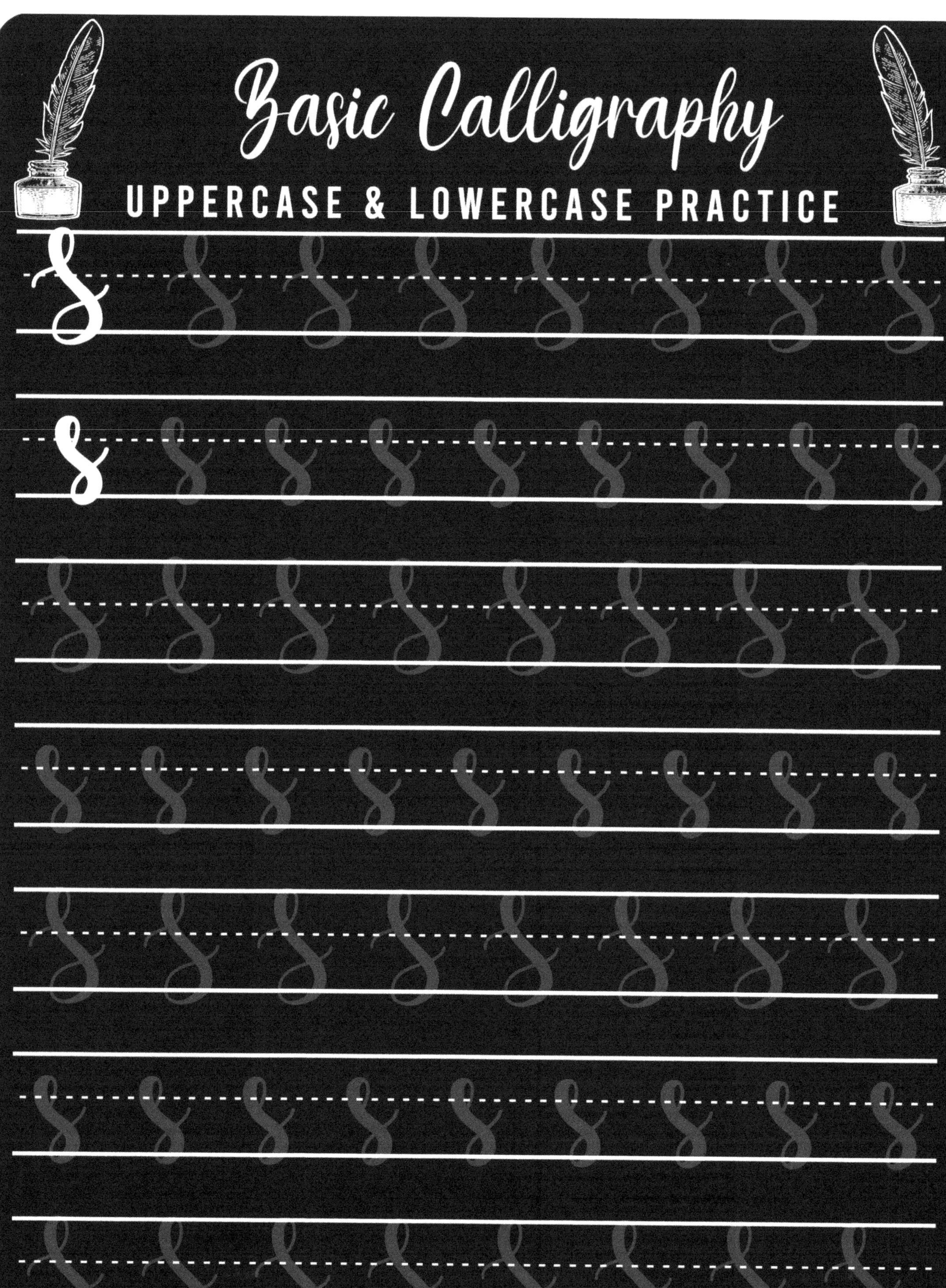

Basic Calligraphy
UPPERCASE & LOWERCASE PRACTICE

# Practice Sheet

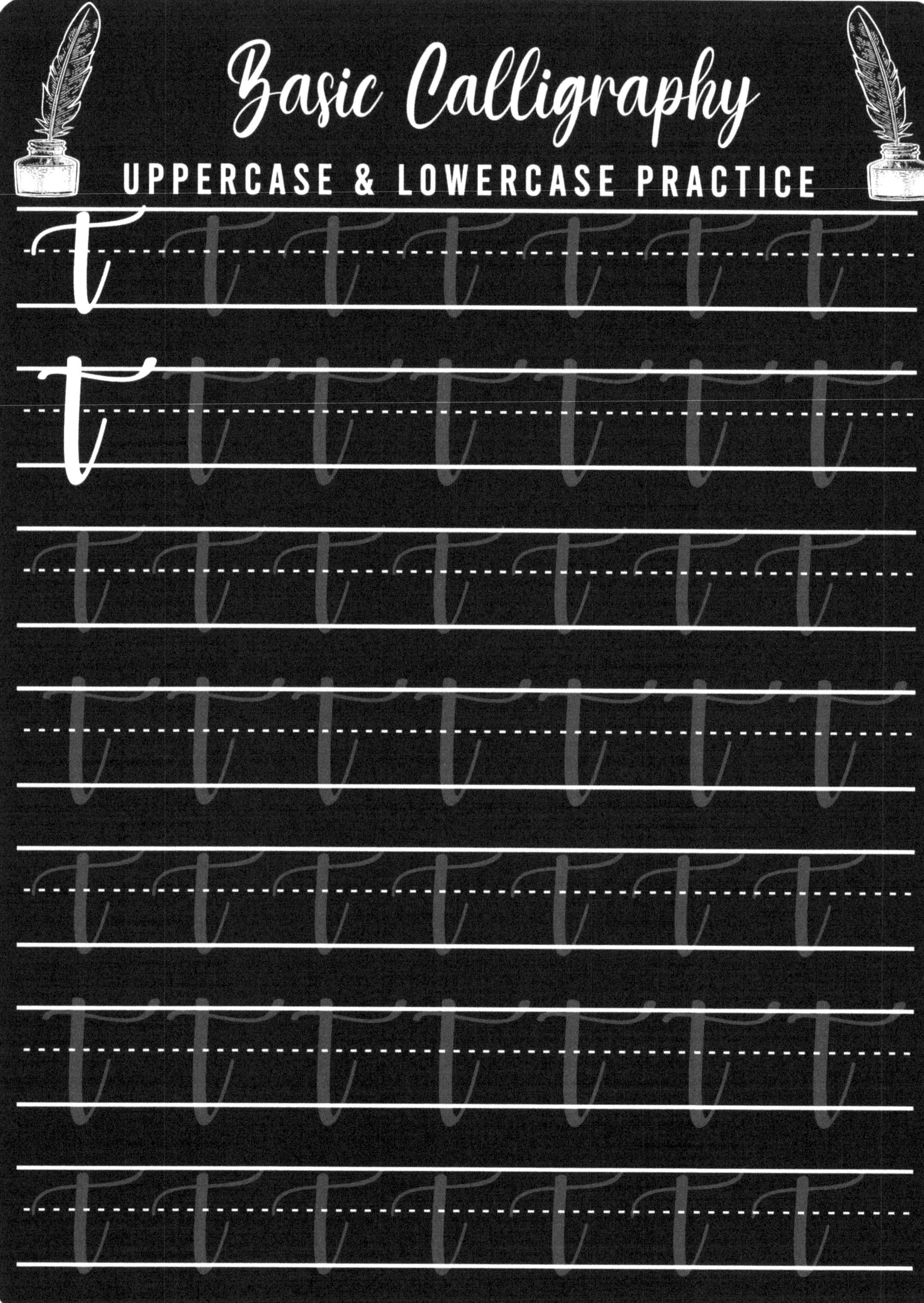

Basic Calligraphy
UPPERCASE & LOWERCASE PRACTICE
T
t

# Practice Sheet

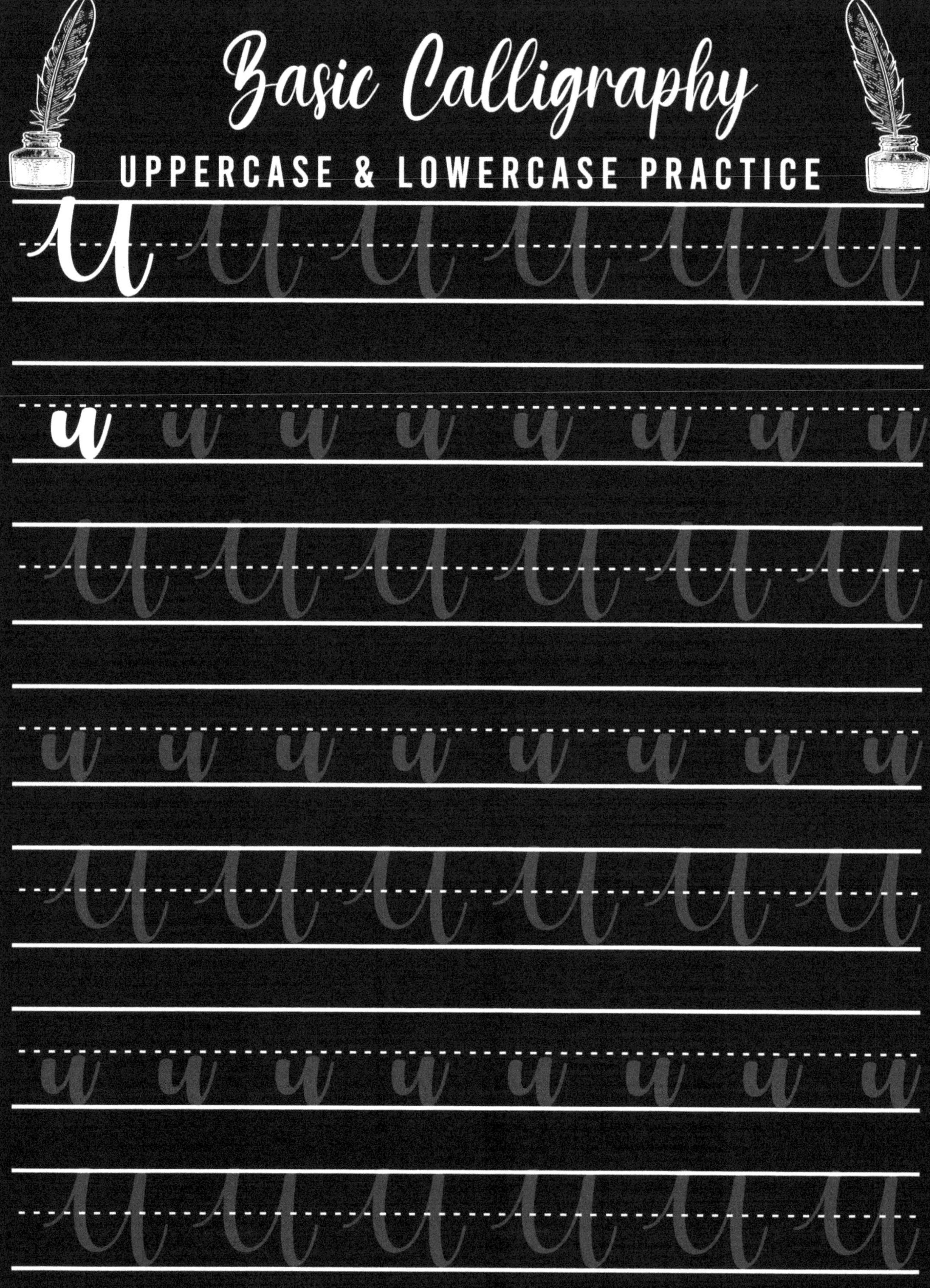
Basic Calligraphy
UPPERCASE & LOWERCASE PRACTICE

# Practice Sheet

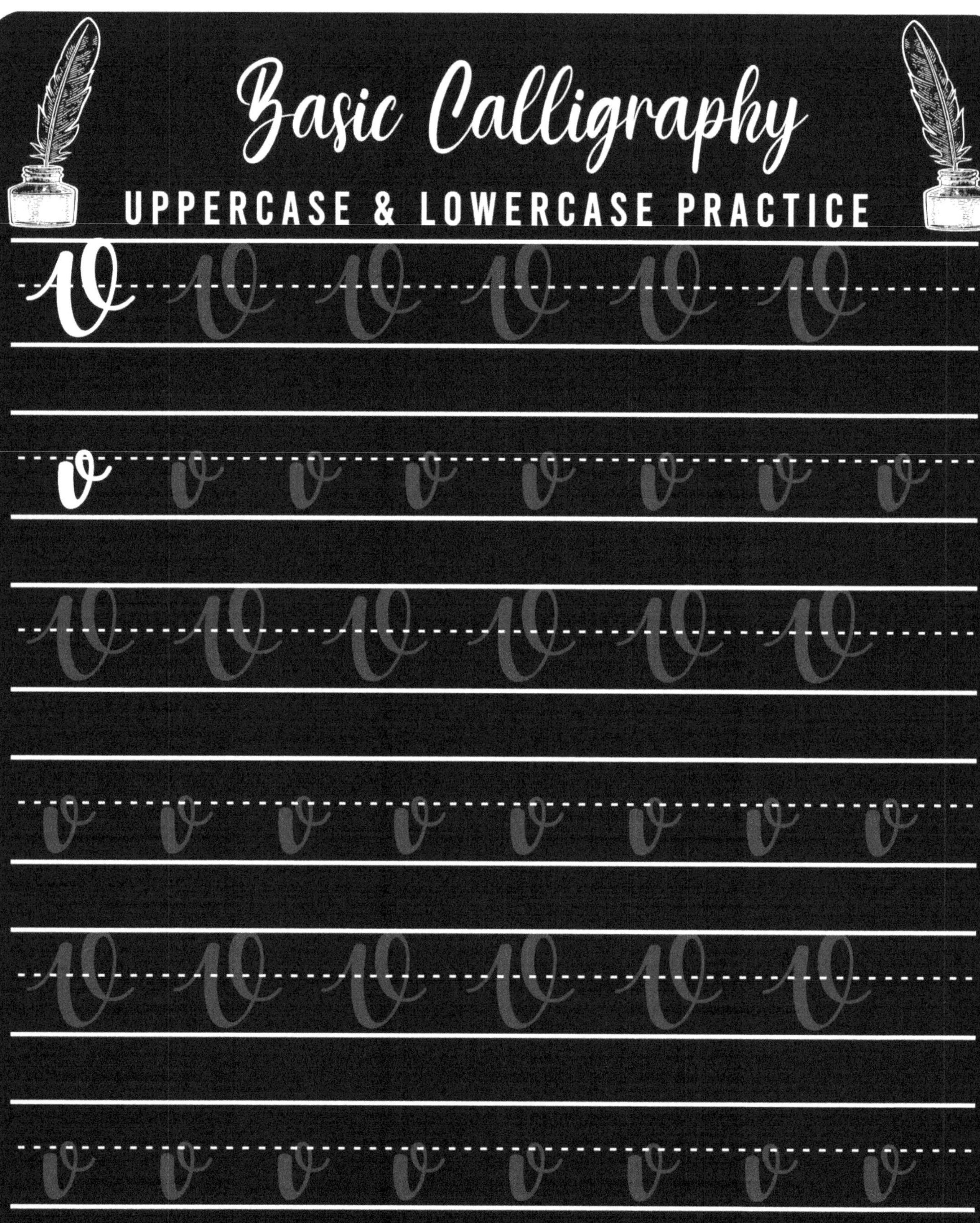
Basic Calligraphy
UPPERCASE & LOWERCASE PRACTICE
V V V V V V
v v v v v v v v
V V V V V V
v v v v v v v v
V V V V V V
v v v v v v v v
V V V V V V

# Practice Sheet

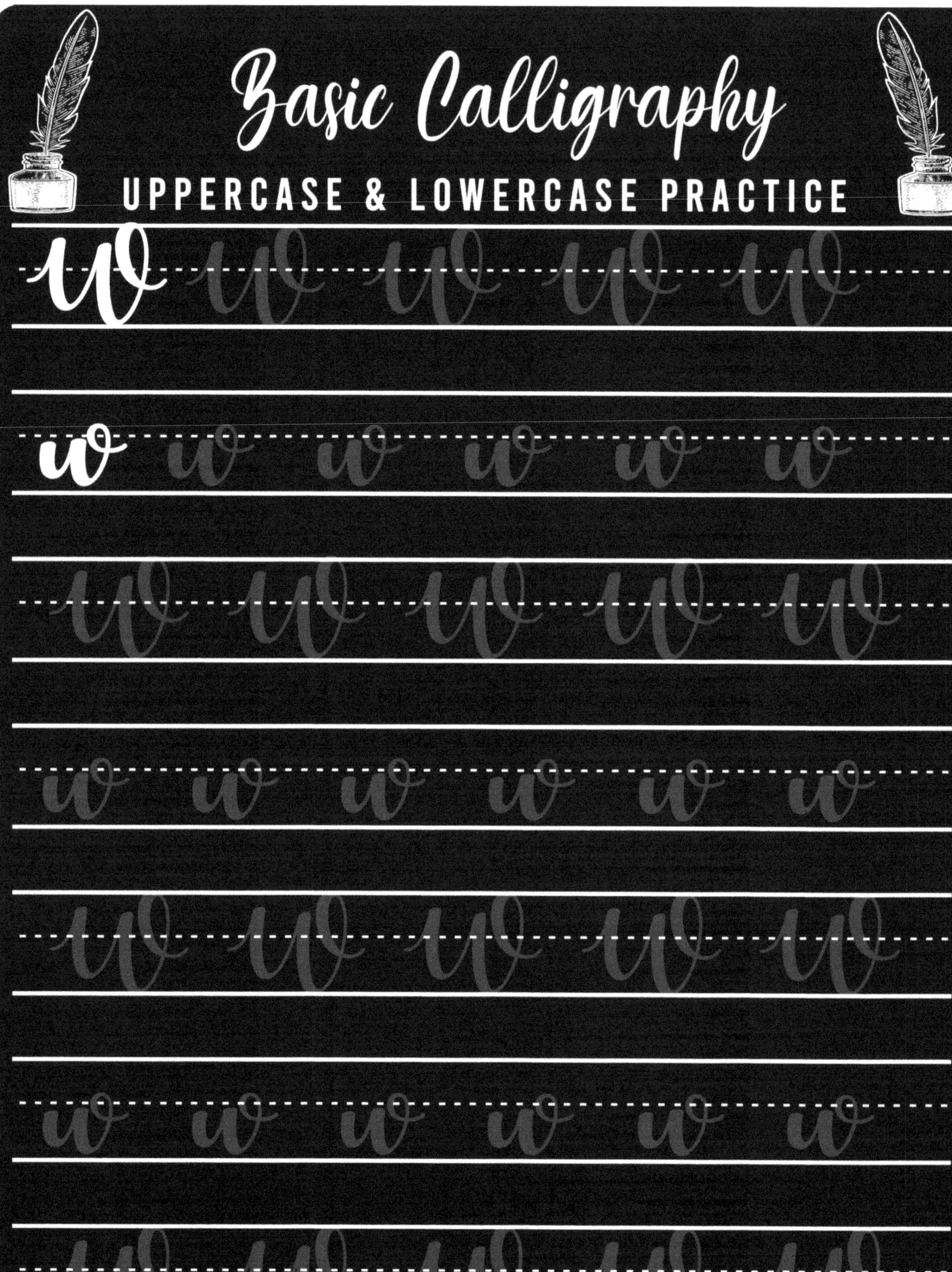
Basic Calligraphy
UPPERCASE & LOWERCASE PRACTICE

# Practice Sheet

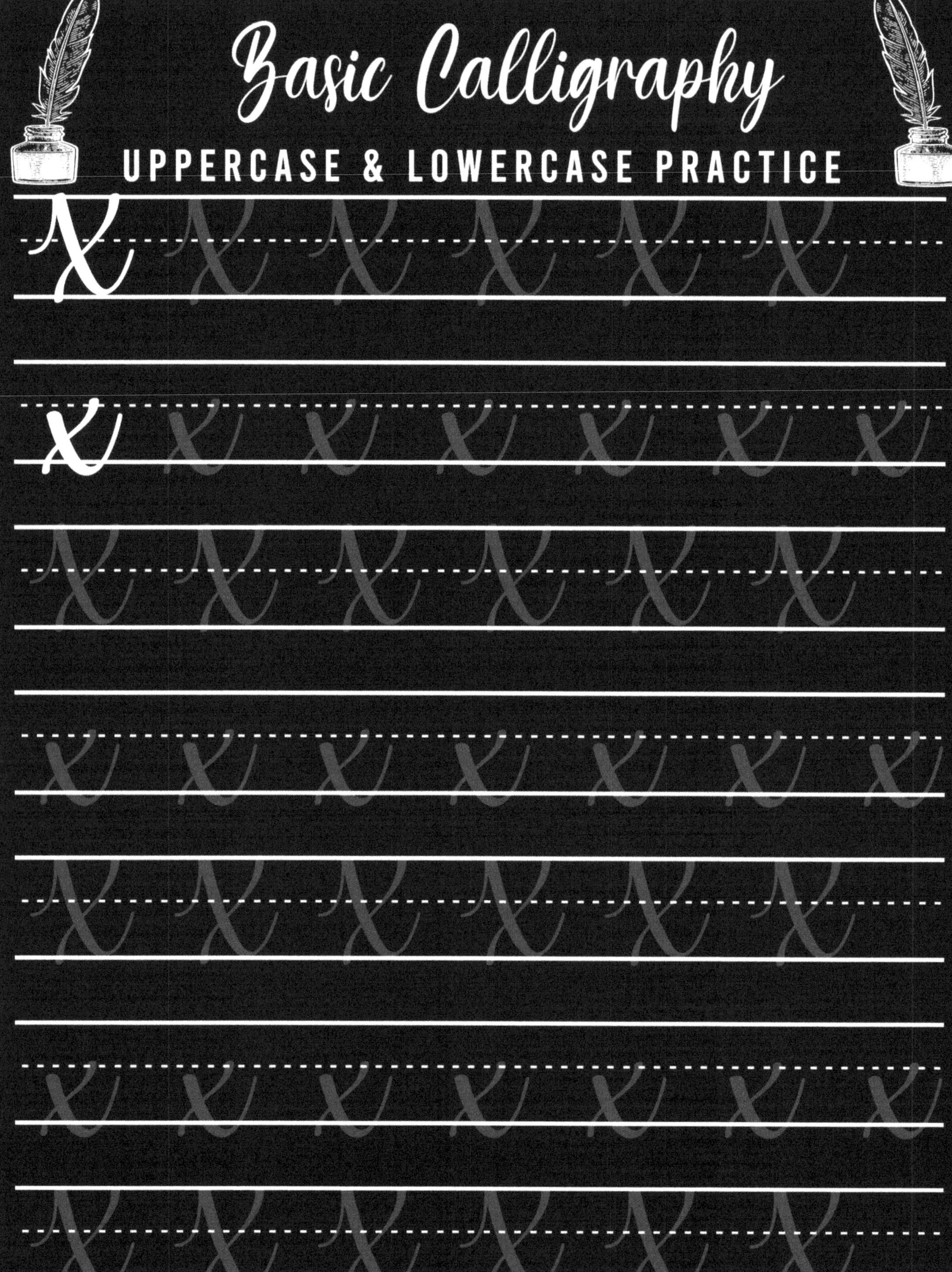
Basic Calligraphy
UPPERCASE & LOWERCASE PRACTICE
X
x

# Practice Sheet

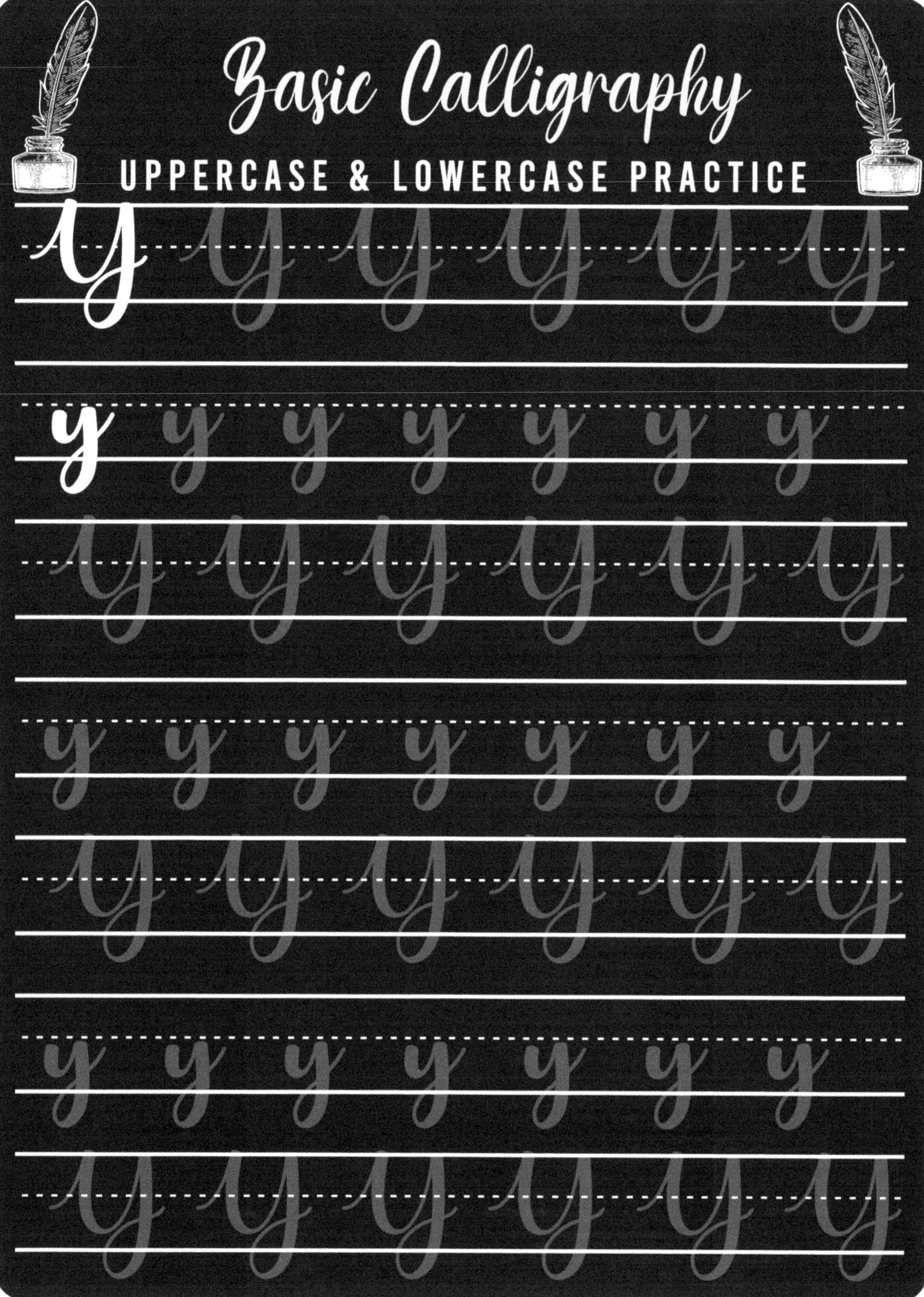

Basic Calligraphy
UPPERCASE & LOWERCASE PRACTICE
Y Y Y Y Y Y Y
y y y y y y y

# Practice Sheet

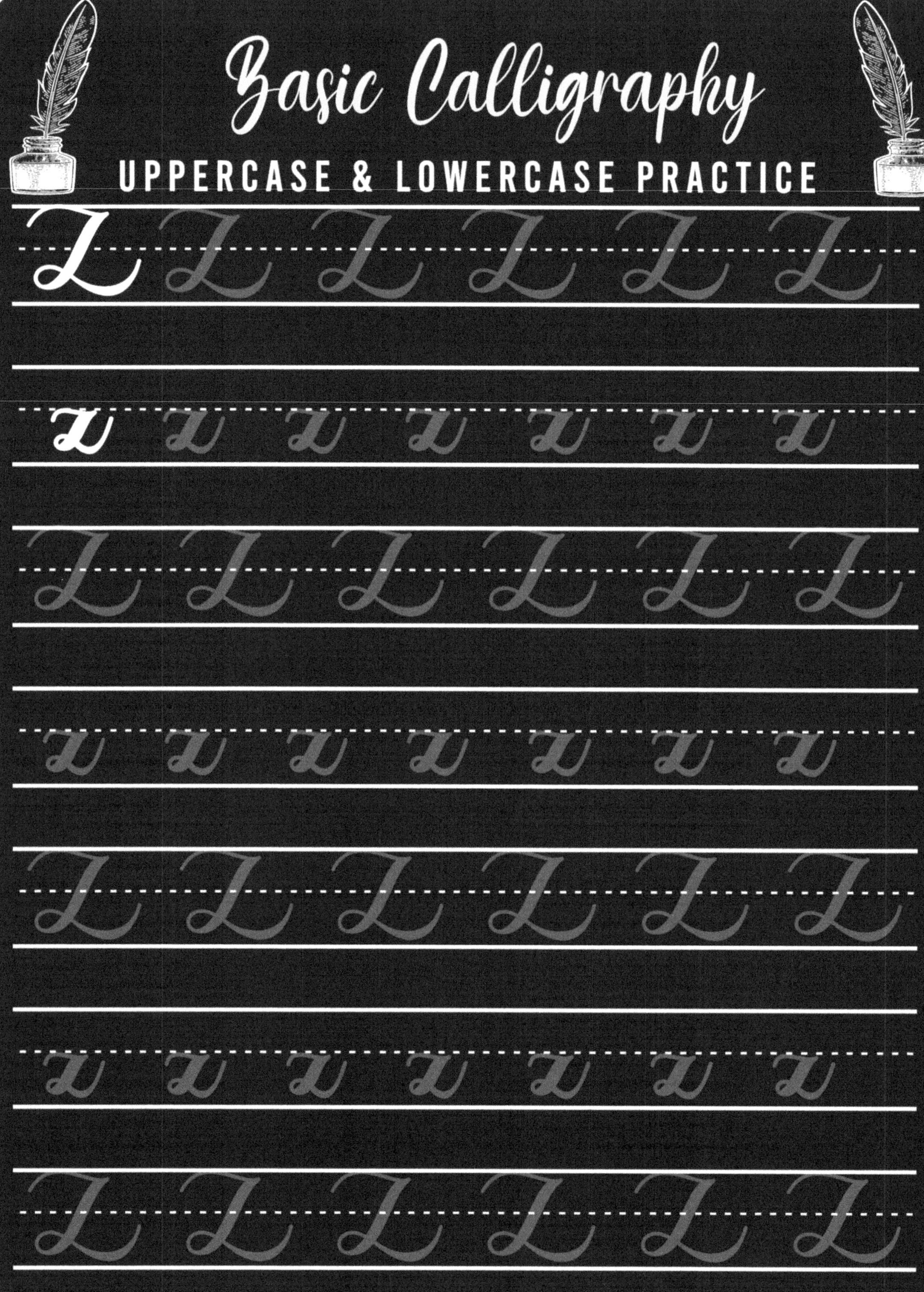
Basic Calligraphy
UPPERCASE & LOWERCASE PRACTICE

# Practice Sheet

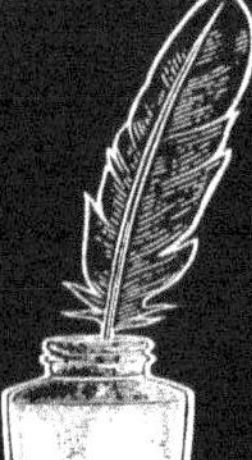

# Connections And Words

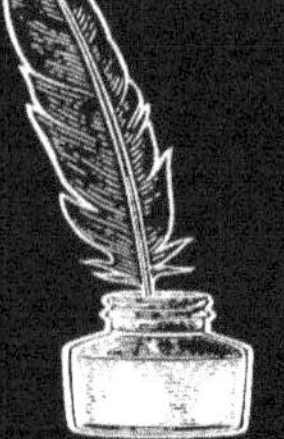

## LOWERCASE BRUSH

You're doing great lettering! Give yourself a pat on the back for making it this far and keeping going. Celebrate your wins.

Don't forget to pick up your pen after each stroke and keep going! You're already a kick butt letterer.

a b : ab ab ab ab

g r : gr gr gr gr

s w : sw sw sw sw

d o : do do do do

m i : mi mi mi mi

l a : la la la la

c h : ch ch ch ch

l l : ll ll ll ll

# Practice Sheet

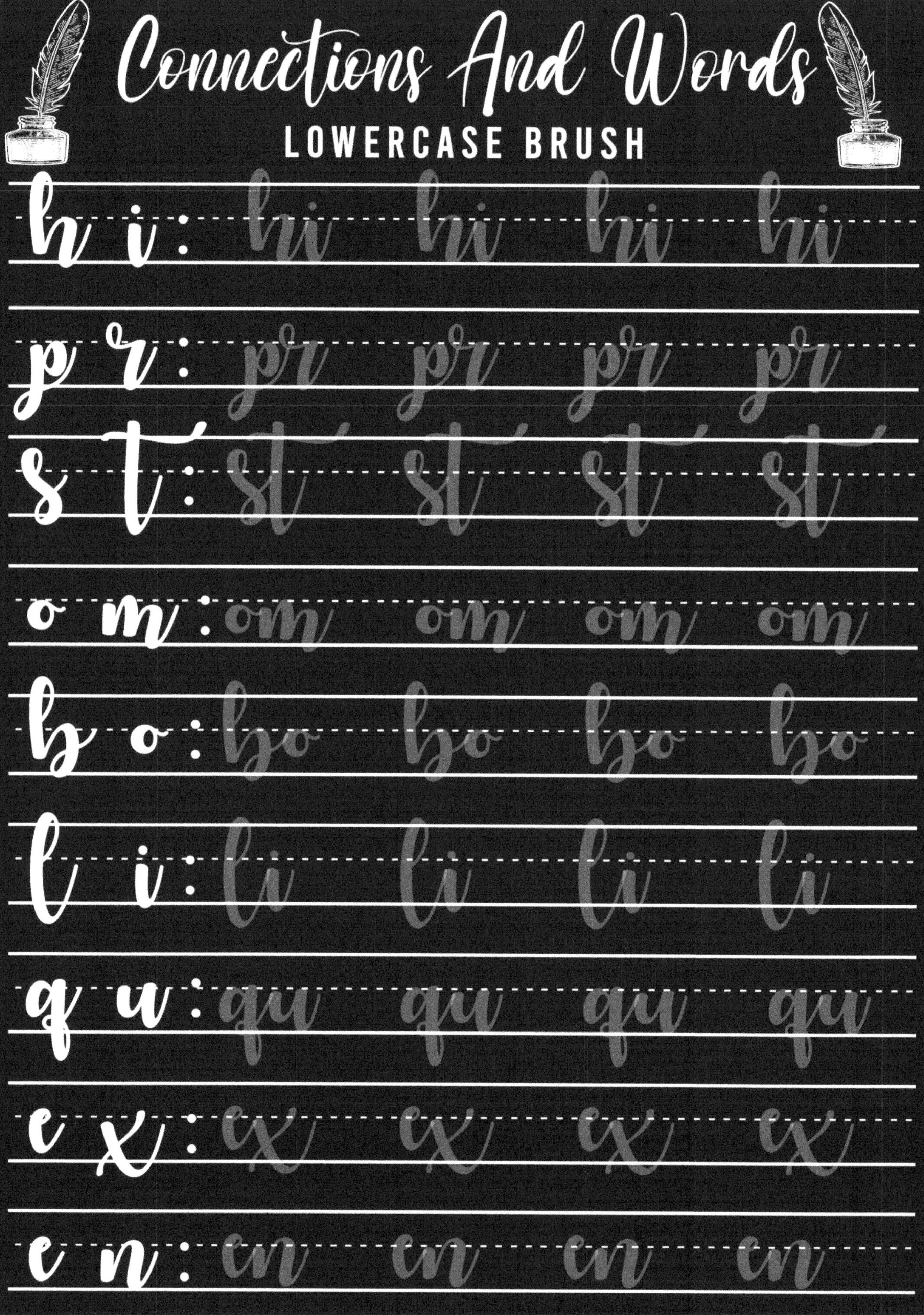
Connections And Words
LOWERCASE BRUSH
h i : hi hi hi hi
p r : pr pr pr pr
s t : st st st st
o m : om om om om
b o : bo bo bo bo
l i : li li li li
q u : qu qu qu qu
e x : ex ex ex ex
e n : en en en en

# Practice Sheet

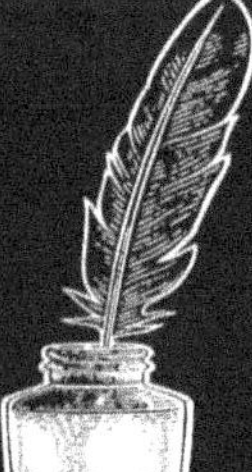

# Connections And Words

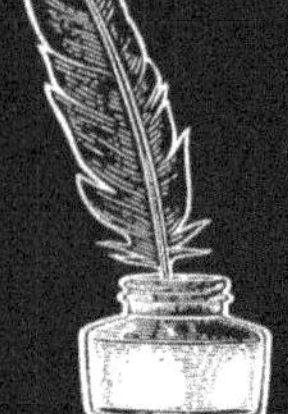

## LOWERCASE BRUSH

You're doing great lettering! Give yourself a pat on the back for making it this far and keeping going. Celebrate your wins.

Don't forget to pick up your pen after each stroke and keep going! You're already a kick butt letterer.

a b : ab ab ab ab

g r : gr gr gr gr

s w : sw sw sw sw

d o : do do do do

m i : mi mi mi mi

l a : la la la la

c h : ch ch ch ch

l l : ll ll ll ll

# Practice Sheet

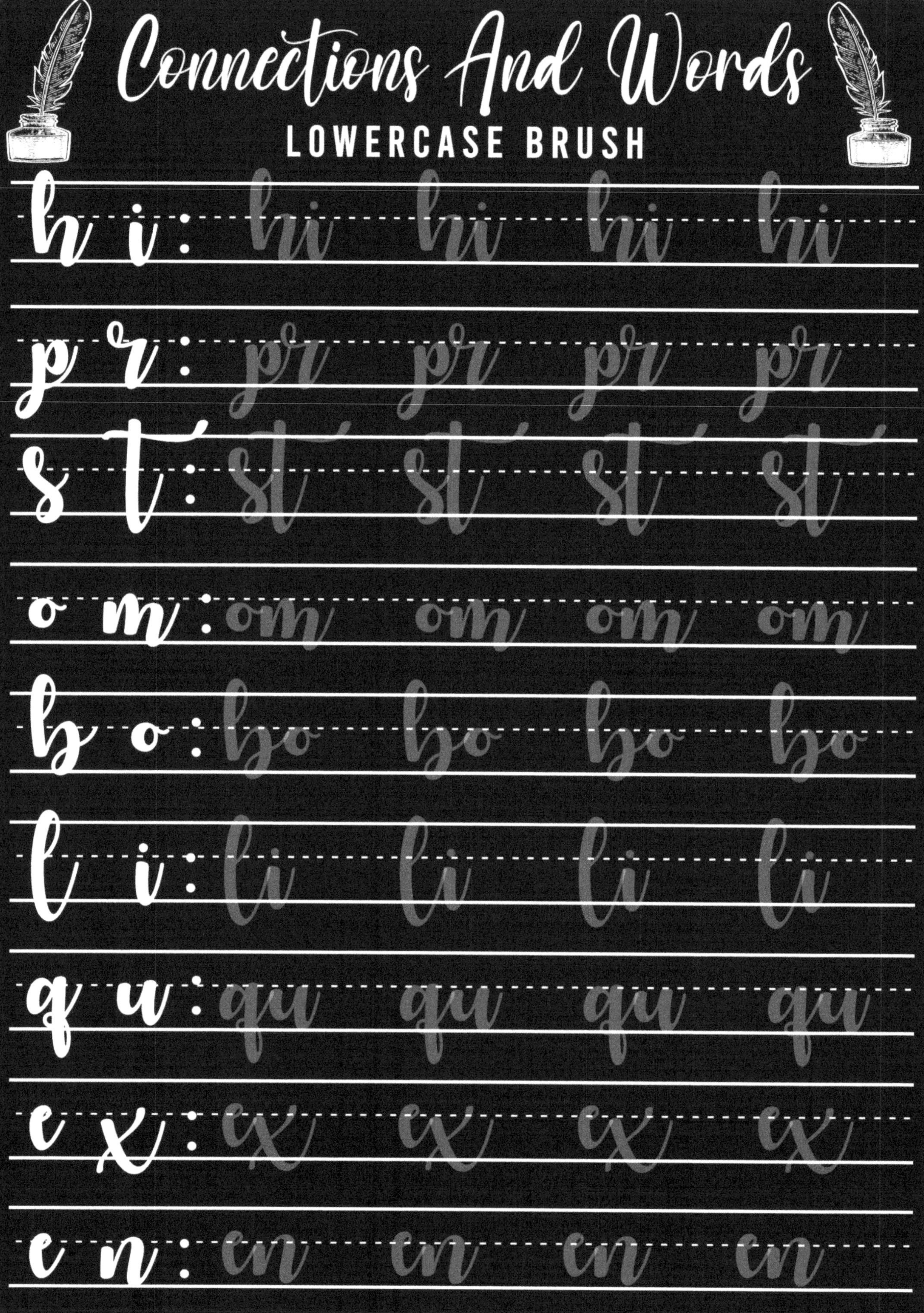
Connections And Words
LOWERCASE BRUSH
h i : hi hi hi hi
p r : pr pr pr pr
s t : st st st st
o m : om om om om
b o : bo bo bo bo
l i : li li li li
q u : qu qu qu qu
e x : ex ex ex ex
e n : en en en en

# Practice Sheet

# Practice Sheet

# Practice Sheet

# Practice Sheet

# Practice Sheet

# Practice Sheet

Practice Sheet

# Practice Sheet

# Practice Sheet

I want to thank You for purchasing This Book. I would be very grateful for taking a moment and leaving feedback. It helps our small business grow and reach more people.

Life Style Daily Team

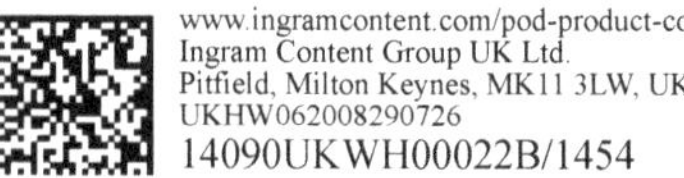

www.ingramcontent.com/pod-product-compliance
Ingram Content Group UK Ltd.
Pitfield, Milton Keynes, MK11 3LW, UK
UKHW062008290726
14090UKWH00022B/1454

9 788367 484596